Tales from Hollywood

A Play

Christopher Hampton

Samuel French—London

New York—Sydney—Toronto—Hollywood

TALES FROM HOLLYWOOD

First produced in Great Britain in the Olivier auditorium of the National Theatre on 1st September, 1983, with the following cast of characters:

Ödön von Horváth	Michael Gambon
Young Man	Michael Mueller
Johnny Weissmuller	Franc Morgan
Thomas Mann	Guy Rolfe
Chico Marx	Roderick Smith
Harpo Marx	Harry Dickman
Greta Garbo	Sylvia Rotter
Charles Money	John Bluthal
Heinrich Mann	Philip Locke
Nelly Mann, his wife	Billie Whitelaw
Salka Viertel	Pamela Buchner
Walter, the butler	Brian Kent
Lion Feuchtwanger	Harry Perscy
Marta Feutchwanger	Annie Leon
Toni Spuhler, the cook	Mary Chester
Katja Mann, Thomas's wife	Sylvia Barter
Helen Schwartz	Barbara Flynn
Bertolt Brecht	Ian McDiarmid
Helene Weigel, his wife	Sylvia Rotter
Hal, the barman	Paul Imbusch
Angel	Belinda Lang
Jacob Lomakhin	John Bluthal
Robert E. Stripling	Paul Stewart
Art Nicely	David Baron
with	Eve Adam
	Audrey Noble

Other parts played by members of the company

Directed by Peter Gill
Designed by Alison Chitty

ACT I 1938-41

ACT II 1942-50

CHARACTERS

Odön von Horváth
Charles Money
Thomas Mann
Heinrich Mann
Helen Schwartz
Nelly Mann
Salka Viertel
Marta Feuchtwanger
Bertolt Brecht
Helene Weigel
Hal
Angel
Jacob Lomakhin
Art Nicely
Voice of Robert E. Stripling

A Young Man
Katja Mann
Lion Feuchtwanger
Toni Spuhler
Walter

And with the friendly participation of:
Johnny Weissmuller
Chico Marx
Harpo Marx
Greta Garbo

PRODUCTION NOTE

This Acting Edition is based on the National Theatre production where elaborate staging facilities were used to ensure rapid, fluent scene changes. Each director will have to evolve settings to suit the facilities available but it is important that the scenes should flow smoothly into each other without interruption.

It will be seen from the text that in Act I scenes 1 and 8 and Act II scene 8 no settings are specified.

Ödön von Horváth (b. 1901) was one of the most talented writers of his generation. He was killed on 1st June 1938, in a freak accident on the Champs Élysées, when a branch of the chestnut tree under which he was sheltering fell on his head.

A colleague, Walter Mehring, who was staying in the same hotel in Paris, went into Horváth's room. On his desk were two half-empty glasses of red wine and a page of notes for the novel (*Adieu Europa*) Horváth was just starting to write. The first line of the notes read: "Ein Poet emigriert nach Amerika . . ."

ACT I*

1938-41

SCENE 1

A curious rippling submarine light

Into it steps a striking figure, fortyish, somewhat overweight, overcoat open to display a well-cut double-breasted grey flannel suit, a Homburg on his head and black shoes, good but scuffed, on his feet, his exophthalmia the most notable feature of his expressive face

He pauses a moment, assessing the audience

Horváth Hello. My name is Ödön von Horváth. (*Pause*) Ödön. (*Pause*) No, Ödön. (*Pause*) Oh, never mind, call me Ed. (*Silence. He listens*) No, that's all right, don't apologize. There's no reason you should ever have heard of me. I had a certain reputation about ten years ago. You know, in the theatre. In Germany. I was considered, you know that word, when they don't really like you but think you might not go away, promising. I had a play in rehearsal when the Nazis came in. It never opened. After that, no-one would put on my plays in Germany, however bad I tried to make them. In the end, I took to writing novels. Also ... but you don't want to hear about all that and I don't want to tell you. Just that through all those years to be a writer in Germany was to be a non-swimmer in the water-polo team.

He moves a few paces, listening. Distant thunder. The underwater effect vanishes and he seems now to be standing under an old-fashioned street light

During the thirties which were also as it happened my thirties, I travelled a good deal. I knew the melancholy of railway stations and the grey wallpaper of cheap hotels. And as the decade, which appeared to have been constructed by a dramatist of the kind many of my more progressive contemporaries were denouncing as hopelessly old-fashioned, as it moved by way of smoothly-plotted climaxes and neatly engineered last minute reversals towards its inevitable conclusion a good many of us, us German writers, I mean, had very narrow escapes. I want to start by telling you about mine. So. (*He pauses*)

Very distant thunder. A light wind, rising

I never had subscribed to the fashionable view that the cinema as an art-form could not survive the coming of sound. On the other hand, I

---

*NB. Paragraph 3 on page ii of this Acting Edition regarding photocopying and video-recording should be carefully read.

hadn't yet had sufficient experience of the medium to realize that the writer's importance to it was somewhere on a par with the hairdresser's.

The Paris crowd are revealed upstage, standing in a line across the stage

Consequently, when I was invited to Paris in May nineteen thirty-eight, to discuss filming one of my novels, I accepted at once. I was still unfamiliar enough with the business to be surprised when at the first meeting, instead of discussing the project, I was bundled into a car, driven to the Champs-Élysées, handed a ticket and sent in to see the latest sensation: *Snow White and the Seven Dwarfs.* Hard to tell what connection it might have had with my novel (which dealt with Nazi education policy) and, given the historical circumstances, I found the film a little optimistic in tone; all the same, in many ways a remarkable piece of work, don't you agree? Afterwards, we had our meeting, which lasted a good ten minutes, at a sidewalk café, and then Siodmak's wife offered to drive me back to my hotel. It was a pleasant evening. I said I would walk.

The crowd briskly walk downstage. Horváth sets off, strolling across the stage, humming "Hi ho, hi ho, it's off to work we go". The wind gets up. A few premonitory drops of rain and then the sound of a solid downpour. The Lights darken downstage. Horváth turns up the collar of his coat

However, I was only half-way down the hill when, out of a clear blue sky, this storm.

Thunderclap

The crowd react and scurry off in all directions

The Young Man moves C *in the shadow of an overhanging branch. We see the glint of his glasses, the shabbiness of his raincoat, and, as he beckons to Horváth, the dull and surprising gleam of an incongruous pair of black leather gloves. Horváth joins him. He has to raise his voice, against the sound of the wind, lashing through the trees*

I joined him in the shelter of an enormous chestnut tree, opposite the *Théâtre Marigny.* Even before he spoke I sensed that he might be, like me, a foreigner, and when he did speak, in better French than I could muster, of the weather, the whereabouts of the nearest bar and the unbearable vulgarity of the Arc de Triomphe, I began to think he might even be a fellow-writer. But before I could ask him, a bizarre commotion occurred.

We hear the sounds, as he describes them

Some way off from where we were standing a tree suddenly snapped in the wind. This fell against our tree, causing a thick branch above our heads to detach itself from the trunk with a slight sucking noise. It then landed on the back of my companion's head.

Without a sound, the Young Man falls to his knees. Then he topples forward on to his face. The back of his head, which is in full light, is crushed like an eggshell. Silence falls, abruptly

Three Men and a Woman rush on immediately. The group freeze as Horváth speaks

He died instantaneously. And this was the incident which prompted me to make the following remark. Why is it people are so afraid of the Nazis? Why aren't they afraid of just walking down the street?

The group come to life again, two of the Men dragging the body by the legs swiftly off, followed by the other Man and Woman

Horváth, having watched the activity, moves downstage and resumes speaking to the audience

I know of no political theory or philosophical system which takes into account the workings of chance. I don't just mean a few centimetres to left or right and it would have been me face down on the stone: I mean that chance, in its most brutal guise, was about to take charge of the lives of millions of Europeans. Not that people realized, of course— I have friends who took taxis to the internment camps. For me, the tree on the Champs-Élysées was enough. And being as I was a German-speaking Hungarian born in an Italian town now part of Yugoslavia, or, as it might be, a native of the sea-coast of Illyria, chance was on my side. Not only did I have a Hungarian passport, I even had a real American uncle, in Lexington, Virginia, who came across right away with the famous affidavit. So while some scrambled desperately for papers which might take them to Mexico City, Helsinki, Shanghai, anywhere, and others sat serenely in Switzerland, while some, calmly or in panic, took their places in the cattle-trucks or swallowed poison in obscure border towns, I was already, flushed with optimism and disregarding certain superstitions I have concerning water, well on the way to ...

Projection: the skyline of New York

Even as I marvelled, though, standing on the deck at dawn, I became aware of a difficulty. For I was a man who, for complicated reasons which took the form of simple fear, was unable to step into an elevator.

The projection fades. Birdsong

Lexington, Virginia, was no better. For my uncle, although in other respects most amiable, was a radio ham and also a member of the Bund. So every evening was spent grappling with the bloody cat's whisker in order to get the full benefit of the Führer's latest thinking.

There is a brief snatch of a Hitler speech, varying wildly in volume and drowned in static, which Horváth abruptly cuts off with a gesture

It seemed there was only one thing for it. Namely ... (*He spreads out his arms*) Los Angeles!

There is an immediate blaze of white light: circus lighting. Horváth begins to wander off

Thomas Mann enters and sits in a wicker chair. He wears a white jacket and a panama hat, glasses and a moustache dyed black, and is about sixty-five

(*As he goes*) Chugging across interminable wheat fields, I dreamed of legendary encounters.

Horváth exits R

Thomas Mann is reading. Quietly in the background a little Wagner plays, the prelude to Lohengrin. *A moment passes. The tranquility is rudely shattered by a familiar ear-splitting cry. Thomas looks up*

Crossing the stage in a great arc, hanging on the end of a rope, a startling apparition: Tarzan. Completing his cry, he lands at Thomas's feet

Thomas looks up at him, his mild expression touched with apprehension and annoyance. Tarzan stretches out his hand. Thomas reluctantly accepts it

Tarzan   Me Johnny Weissmuller, you Thomas Mann.

The Wagner snaps out

Tarzan and Thomas Mann exit. Chico and Harpo Marx enter

The Lights cross fade to Chico and Harpo Marx. Harpo is in baggy white trousers and carries a tennis racquet

Chico   Who wuza this little guy you wuza playin' tennis with?

Harpo shakes his head; disconsolate expression

He beat you, uh?

Harpo nods, tearful

Who wuz he?

Harpo draws his racquet, which has a motor-horn on the end of it, across an imaginary violin

Heifetz?

Harpo drops to one knee. His sneakers have no toecaps. He counts out silently; six toes to each foot

What?

Same routine

He gotta twelve toes? No wunna he beat you. What's his name?

Harpo works his jaw furiously. Chico is puzzled. As the excitement of the question-and-answer session mounts, Harpo punctuates it with blasts on the motor-horn

Teeth?

Harpo shakes his head

Moosejaw?

Harpo shakes his head. His jaw now working frantically, he takes an imaginary something out of his mouth and sticks it behind his ear

Chewinagum?

Harpo nods; then shakes his head. Continuing to chew, he begins to flap imaginary wings

Ostrich?

Harpo shakes his head; begins to move around the stage chewing and flapping his wings

Chicklet?

He's pleased with this, but Harpo shakes his head, exhibiting terrible frustration; he redoubles his efforts

Chewinaboid?

Harpo nods, delighted: congratulatory blasts on the horn. Chico, however, is puzzled again

Chewinaboid? Chewinaboid? I don't know no Chewinaboid.

Harpo holds up a finger for silence. Then, magically, he strums on his tennis racquet, the four regular, melancholy, opening notes of "Verklärte Nacht". Chico's expression clears

Ah! Arnold Schönberg!

Harpo nods ecstatically

Why didn't you say so inna the foist place?

Harpo frowns. Chico throws an arm round him and begins to lead him off

You gotta be careful with him, he gotta very sneaky rhythm.

Chico and Harpo exit. As they do so, Horváth enters upstage, arm-in-arm with a staggeringly beautiful woman: Greta Garbo. They are hotly pursued by several reporters and photographers. Horváth is now dressed for California

They advance downstage, looking deep into each other's eyes. Suddenly, a flashbulb pops. Then, the flashes of what must be dozens of cameras. Garbo breaks away from Horváth, holding up a hand. The flashbulbs stop

Garbo Ve vant to be alone.

The flashbulbs start up again

Garbo turns, looks at Horváth for a moment, then runs off, distraught, hotly pursued by the media

Horváth looks after her, sadly. The Lights change to normal California daytime. Horváth smiles and turns to the audience

Horváth Well. Thomas Mann did know Johnny Weissmuller. Schönberg did

play tennis with Harpo Marx. And I did meet Garbo. But I need hardly
say the reality was very different.

SCENE 2

Charles Money's office

*The Lights come up on Charles Money, sitting behind a desk innocent of
books, but with a great many telephones deployed on it. He is a shortish,
overweight man of middle years*

He looks up as Horváth is shown into his office

*In the scenes where he is with other émigrés, or simply addressing the audience,
Horváth has no accent. However, in his scenes with Americans, his accent is
very strong, and although it will improve as time passes and the play goes
on, as will his use of English, it will always remain very noticeable in these
scenes*

Money struggles to his feet, extending a plump hand

Money Hi.

Horváth shakes his hand, bowing slightly

Horváth Mr Money.
Money Chuck.

Horváth looks around uncertainly, not at all sure what he means by this

Good of you to find the time, Mr Horváth.

He mispronounces the name horrendously. Horváth winces

Horváth Ödön.
Money Uh?
Horváth Ed.
Money Oh, yeah, good.

*The telephone rings. Money turns to answer one of the many telephones on
his desk*

   (*On the telephone*) I'm in a meeting. Oh, Christ, all right. (*To Horváth,
gesturing*) Ed. Sit.

Horváth sits in the chair by the desk

   (*Sitting; effusively into the receiver*) Jack! How are you! ... End of next
week, Jack, I told you ... Yes, I know that, but ... (*Silence, during
which he puts his hand over the receiver*) Talking to this guy is like
drowning in cold gravy. (*Back into the receiver*) Well, I really appreciate
your patience on this, Jack ... She's fine, how's Eileen? ... Yeah, nice
talking to you. (*He puts the receiver down, a trace shaken*) Have you
seen *The Adventures of Robin Hood*?

Horváth This is a film?
Money You haven't seen *The Adventures of Robin Hood*?
Horváth No.
Money Oh.

A different telephone rings. Money picks up the receiver. Brief silence

Of course it's raining. I can see it's fuckn raining! (*He slams down the receiver, irate, takes a moment to collect himself*) You worked for Fox over in Europe, is that right, Ed?
Horváth Yes.
Money And my people tell me you wrote a play about Edward the Second.
Horváth Please?
Money Play. Theatre play. You wrote a play. About Edward Second. English king.
Horváth No.
Money No?
Horváth No.
Money Oh.

Silence

Horváth Ah, I know that, what you mean. *Eduard der Zweite*. Yes. No. This play was from Bertolt Brecht und Lion Feuchtwanger.
Money You didn't have anything to do with it?
Horváth No.

Money considers for a moment

Money Either of them in town, you happen to know?
Horváth No. Mr Feuchtwanger is in France and Mr Brecht is, I think, in Denmark or so.
Money But you are familiar with the material?
Horváth Sorry? My English.
Money Do you know the play?
Horváth Oh. Yes. But in any case is it an old English play.
Money What's that?
Horváth Yes. From Christopher Marlowe.

Silence. Money broods

And I don't think he is in town either.

No reaction to this from Money, who continues to reflect, frowning

Money Let me have it run for you.
Horváth I'm sorry?
Money *The Adventures of Robin Hood*. It was huge. It did three million domestic. It'll give you an idea.
Horváth For what?
Money Listen, let me explain. These things nobody can explain. But for some reason right now English history is very hot. So somebody came

up with this Edward the Second idea, and what we have here is a
treatment. (*He hands Horváth a slim folder*)
Horváth Thank you.
Money It's a way of presenting the facts we think may work, but you
don't have to take any notice of it, hell, you're the writer.
Horváth Yes.

Money frowns

Money You a member of the Screenwriters' Guild?
Horváth No. You want I become a membership?
Money No, no, that's fine.

Silence. Money stares at him for a moment

OK, Ed, I'm prepared to offer you a hundred dollars a week.

Horváth makes a gesture, wearily assenting

Half now, half on delivery.
Horváth But ...?
Money You need two weeks?
Horváth Maybe.
Money OK, you got it. End of next week, then. (*He smiles. Then a thought
strikes him and the smile disappears*) You OK to write in English?
Horváth (*eagerly*) Oh, sure. I am taking lessons.
Money Good.
Horváth Yes. I am now knowing three thousand words of English.
Money Congratulations.
Horváth Excuse me?

*A telephone rings. Money selects a receiver and listens. Horváth abruptly
turns to the audience, rises and moves downstage as he speaks. His accent
has disappeared. In the background, the Lights go down on Money, as he
listens on the telephone. A spot follows Horváth*

The telephone. They even have some damned bird out here sounds like
a telephone. That week Hitler marched into Czechoslovakia. *Variety*
said: Hitler's reshuffling of Central Europe represents a loss of two and
a half to three per cent of total foreign film income.

SCENE 3

Thomas Mann's bungalow

Horváth These mundane tasks were interrupted by a summons to Parnas-
sus. The Nobel Prize-winner was passing through on one of his
lecture-tours, speaking on "The Problems of Freedom" or some such
burning topic. I had, of course, met Thomas Mann often during the
twenties, in Germany, but this was the first evening I ever spent with
him alone.

The Lights come up on Thomas Mann, comfortably installed in his bungalow at the Beverly Hills Hotel, *pouring himself a cup of coffee.* Horváth *joins him, picking up a glass of brandy on his way*

Pleasant as it was to be able to speak my own language again, the occasion was not without its mishaps. (*He sits in the armchair*)

Thomas Mann lights a cigarette, carefully

Thomas What did you think of my lecture? Be honest.
Horváth I shall have to be very honest. I'm afraid I missed it.
Thomas Oh?
Horváth I have a deadline coming up, my first American screenplay.
Thomas I hope I'm not keeping you from it now.
Horváth Also, I wasn't quite sure if I would be able to follow your English.
Thomas My English is very good.
Horváth Oh, yes, it's mine that's terrible. I took some lessons in Vienna but I had to give them up.
Thomas Why?
Horváth They made me feel like a head waiter.

Thomas Mann relaxes, somewhat mollified. He drinks some coffee

Thomas What does it deal with, this screenplay of yours?
Horváth Edward the Second of England. Based on Marlowe's play.
Thomas Interesting. Did you ever see Brecht's version?
Horváth No.
Thomas Oh, I did. About fifteen years ago in Berlin. I remember it vividly. It was dreadful.
Horváth In what way?
Thomas Everything so relentlessly ugly. Costumes made out of old sacks. They kept complaining about the king's extravagance, and then on he'd come wearing something they'd just shaken the potatoes out of. Even the king's boyfriend was the most unattractive lump in the company. And quite deliberately so. I don't begin to understand that Brecht, do you? Of course, as you know, in my book *Buddenbrooks*, the dentist is called Herr Brecht, so I've never been able to take him quite seriously, his name doesn't have the right resonance. I feel much more comfortable with your work.
Horváth Well...
Thomas That first charming little book of yours, you know the one I mean, I thought it was remarkable. No-one else has been able to write like that about life inside the Third Reich. How did you manage to find out all those things?
Horváth I... I've kept up my contacts with people inside Germany.
Thomas Well, so have we all. But I couldn't write about what it is to live there. You're very bold.
Horváth Well, you know, I... at the beginning, I went back quite often.
Thomas Really?

Horváth Oh, yes, I even, I meant to tell you this, at the book-burning, the great book-burning in Berlin, I was there.

Thomas I don't see how you could possibly have been.

Horváth I saw them all filing past Goebbels in their academic robes, heaving books on to the bonfire, and that professor, what's his name, Bäumler, I saw him dance. I heard him shouting: "Burn, Thomas Mann, burn!", yelling like a bad actor.

Silence. Mann is shaken

Then Goebbels made a speech and said: "Tonight, the intellect awakes". I watched the whole thing.

Thomas Weren't they burning your books too?

Horváth No, no, I'm not well-known enough. The compensations of obscurity.

Thomas It's true. Fame carries very heavy obligations.

Horváth I'm sure.

Thomas I often wonder, you know, if we writers have done enough to prevent the world from rolling to the brink of war.

Horváth Oh, my family has a very poor record when it comes to preventing wars. My father, who was a diplomat, had a meeting with the Archduke Franz Ferdinand in the spring of nineteen fourteen. His highness said he was planning a tour of Bosnia. My father assured him this was an excellent idea and particularly recommended a visit to Sarajevo. So all this is really his fault.

Thomas Forgive me if I can't bring myself to smile. Ever since that monster destroyed Czechoslovakia ... my brother Heinrich and I are Czech citizens now, you know, the government granted us special passports. I blame perfidious Albion, of course. How can that cretinous weakling Chamberlain suppose that letting Hitler do as he pleases is less dangerous than negotiating with the Communists? If he'd stood firm, none of this would ever have happened, Hitler would have fallen ... and I would not have been placed in the intolerable position of having to advocate war. That's enough of that. Have you a new book ready for us?

Horváth Yes. It's called *Europe, Goodbye.*

Thomas Will you read some of it to me? Do you have it with you?

Horváth No. No, I don't.

Thomas Oh, what a disappointment.

Silence. Thomas Mann seems to be waiting for something

Horváth Perhaps ... would you read something of yours?

Thomas (*picking up a thick manuscript off the table*) Well, all right, if you insist, certainly. My voice is a little tired from lecturing, but ...

Horváth Well, then, please don't ...

Thomas No, no, if you insist. At the moment, I'm writing about Goethe. This was intended to be a *Novelle*, but these things have a habit of expanding out of my grasp. I don't have your enviable gift of brevity any more.

Horváth Some would say I'm short-winded.

Thomas Oh, come, come. Now, where are we? (*He shuffles through the manuscript*). Of course, at this critical point of history, it may seem criminally irresponsible to spend one's energies painting a portrait of some long-dead German writer, however great . . .

Pause. Thomas Mann waits

Horváth Oh, I don't see why.

Thomas But one must obey the dictates of one's instinct. It takes years for the secret significance of a work of art to reveal itself to the artist himself, let alone to his public.

Horváth Well, I must say your story *Death in Venice* has taken on a special meaning for me in recent years.

Thomas No doubt on the grounds of its convenient length.

Horváth No. No. Not on those grounds.

Thomas I started work, for instance, on my *Joseph* book in 'twenty-three. Who could have imagined then how relevant the theme of an intellectual in exile would become? The laws of art are truly unfathomable. We have no choice but to obey them, even if we can never understand them. (*He picks up the manuscript again and puts on his glasses*)

Horváth turns to address the audience

Horváth I agreed that the laws of art were whatever it was he'd said they were. He began to read.

Thomas reads out loud. After a moment, Horváth puts Money's "treatment" down on the coffee table, gets up and moves downstage. Thomas's voice fades and the Lights on the bungalow slowly fade to Black-out. A spot follows Horváth

He read from his imperishable masterpiece, *Lotte In Weimar*. But the sinuous elaboration of his syntax, the lulling sonorities of his laureate's voice were such that, regrettably, within a very few minutes, I was sound asleep.

Scene 4

Charles Money's office

Horváth I delivered my script and was asked to call back the following day. Only the kind collaboration of Christopher Marlowe had enabled me, in the time allotted, to complete a piece of work in a foreign language. I made the play as filmic as I could, but almost all the words were Marlowe's. I returned, quietly confident.

The Lights come up on Money sitting glowering behind his desk. Horváth approaches, smiling

Mr Money.

Money rises and picks up a heavy black folder, which he instantly hurls

*across the room at Horváth. They look at each other for a moment. Horváth's
expression is quizzical*

Money (*suddenly shouting*) Whaddya think that is?

Silence. Horváth picks up the folder and studies it briefly

Horváth Well, heavens to Betsy, it's my script.

Money Script! You wouldn't get that on fuckn radio!

Silence. Money paces up and down. Horváth watches him with mild interest

How could you do this to me, Ed?

Horváth Do what?

Money I put my ass on the line for you. Have you any idea what kind of
trouble I'm in now?

Horváth No.

Money Well, now, Ed, this is going to be a very short meeting. But you're
new in town and I think I'd better straighten you out.

Horváth Am I bent?

A telephone rings before Money can answer. He picks up the receiver

Money (*shouting into the telephone*) No! Five minutes! (*He slams the receiver down and looks up at Horváth*) Listen, Ed, I know your English is
bad, you can't help that, but this is a goddamn disaster area.

Horváth Well, I used the Marlowe ...

Money I don't care if you used fuckn Webster's, Ed, English this ain't.

Horváth I see.

Money Another thing. You can't even type right. The whole script is laid
out like some goddamn poem.

Horváth You want me, that I explain ...

Money No, I don't want you, that you explain. All I'm saying is, you
want Ty Power and Linda Darnell to read your script you do not bring
them fuckn *Hiawatha*.

Horváth This I understand.

Money's tone changes abruptly to one of solicitude

Money I gave you a treatment, Ed, why didn't you work from the treatment?

Horváth Excuse me?

Money The treatment!

Horváth Oh. Yes, I threw this away. I thought it was unbelievable wulgar.

Money Vulgar! Wait a minute, Ed, I wrote that.

Horváth shrugs. Money's rage is mounting again

Vulgar! Listen, when I read your script, I pass over the fact it was in
pidgin English, there was this stuff, I couldn't believe it, I had to go
back and read it again, but there it was, I've never seen anything like it
in the script of a major motion picture, in your story the King of
England is a goddamn faggot!

Horváth A faggot?
Money A faggot, a fruit, a ... homosexual!
Horváth Ah. But this is historic true.
Money Are you crazy? So what? Listen, for all I know Robin Hood liked
to do it with sheep, you think anyone wants to see that? This is for
family audiences, not for the back room of the cathouse. This is an
adventure picture, not the goddamn ballet. You come to me with some
piece of shit has the King of England climbing into bed with a boy and
you tell me I'm vulgar? Jesus fucking Christ!
Horváth So I am how you say fired.
Money You bet your ass.
Horváth Then I say good-day.

Money calms down as Horváth starts to leave

Money Wait a minute.

Horváth waits

I don't know what you do in Europe, Ed, I don't know the kind of
material Fox goes for over there. All I'm telling you is you can't pull
this kind of stunt in this country. We're not ready for it.

A telephone rings. Money picks up the receiver angrily

Didn't you hear what I said? ... Oh ... oh, Jack ... Yeah, listen, I have
a little problem ...

*As he speaks, Horváth leaves the room. The Lights go down on Money, as
Horváth approaches the audience*

Horváth I couldn't find it in my heart to be too angry with Herr Money.
Later on, of course, I realized what had really been happening: he was
a writer-producer, and he'd subcontracted me, at a fraction of his own
salary, to do a job he was supposed to be doing himself. Anyway, at
least he paid me, despite his horror at European morals, which is more
than I can say for some later employers, however amiable their manner.
So. First blood to Hollywood.

SCENE 5

The Warner Brothers' commissary

Horváth I had earned a reasonable amount of money in my youth, but all
of it had disappeared on train fares and hotel rooms, in bars and taxi
cabs and coffee houses. Now I discovered that in contrast to many parts
of Europe, this was a country in which it was difficult to be poor with
dignity. However, the inconveniences I suffered were as nothing compared to those of my friends who were still in Europe. The governments
of Britain and France, entirely ignoring the misgivings of *Variety*, had
declared war on Germany. Individuals in America were making heroic

efforts to help those trapped in Occupied Europe, but at the same time chance was sharpening the knives on its chariot-wheels. The man the State Department put in charge of the refugee problem was a former Ambassador to Rome who had been enormously impressed by the punctuality of Mussolini's trains, and who thought anyone who mismanaged their life to the extent of becoming a refugee was deeply suspicious, probably undesirable and, as often as not, a Jew. I, on the other hand, was a beneficiary of all this frenzied activity. An organization was formed, called the European Film Fund, to provide work in Hollywood for needy émigré writers. And so it was that I found myself an employee of: (*he indicates the projection screen*)

Projection: The Warner Brothers' logo; music: signature tune from Looney Tunes

Truth to tell, when it came to devising something for all their new writers to do, the Brothers found themselves somewhat at a loss. So the corridors of the writers' building were jammed with bewildered Germans asking each other how they ought to be treating their secretaries.

The Lights come up on a corner of the Warner Brothers' commissary. Also, way upstage and not in light, is the indistinct figure of an old man, Heinrich Mann, slightly hunched, waiting, as if lost or abandoned, not moving. In the commissary, sitting alone at a corner table, reading, drinking black coffee, is a slight, dark woman in her late twenties, Helen Schwartz

One day, in the rest room, I was amazed to find standing next to me, Heinrich Mann, Thomas Mann's elder brother. As he had always been something of a hero of mine, I invited him to join me in the commissary for a coffee.

Horváth moves upstage to collect Heinrich Mann. He is sixty-nine, a dignified figure, somewhat heavier in build than his brother, but with the same neat moustache and round glasses. His clothes are old but good, incongruously formal for the setting, a handkerchief carefully arranged in his breast pocket. He moves with Horváth, into the commissary. Helen looks up when they arrive, then back at her book. Heinrich installs himself at a table

Horváth goes off, returning immediately with coffee on a tray, and still holding the manuscript

As he's unloading the tray, he's staring at Helen. She looks up and sees him. Instead of turning away, he smiles at her. She nods, in brusque acknowledgement, frowning slightly. Horváth sits down next to Heinrich, who's just taking a sip of coffee

Heinrich Not coffee as we think of it, of course, but then in France, these last few months, it wasn't to be found anywhere.
Horváth Hard to imagine France without coffee.
Heinrich I would have been happy to spend the rest of my life in France.

Silence

Tell me, what is it they expect us to do here?

Horváth Keep out of their way, I think, I don't know.

Heinrich But we're supposed to be writing scenarios, is that right?

Horváth Theoretically.

Heinrich What are scenarios?

Horváth Oh, stories you think might work well as films.

Heinrich People keep asking me to go to, what are they called, the film-shows here?

Horváth Screenings.

Heinrich Screenings, yes, and I sit and watch them, but I never know why they ask me.

Horváth They want to know what you think of them.

Heinrich Oh, I always say the same thing. Very good.

Horváth Even if they're terrible?

Heinrich Yes. Unless they're completely terrible.

Horváth Then what do you say?

Heinrich I say very interesting.

Horváth I don't think you need my advice.

Heinrich They always introduce me as the man who wrote *The Blue Angel*.

Horváth Ah, yes.

Heinrich At first, I used to say, I didn't write it, I wrote a novel thirty-five years ago, on which the film is very loosely based. They changed the ending, I would say. Then I understood they didn't want to hear that. So now I say, did you like it oh I'm so glad thank you very much.

Horváth I'm sure you're right.

Heinrich Yes. My entire American reputation stands on the legs of Marlene Dietrich.

Horváth Surely not.

Heinrich When I arrived in New York last month with my nephew Golo, the *New York Times* welcomed the arrival of the famous German author, Golo Mann. Then they said he was accompanied by his Uncle Heinrich.

Horváth I can't believe it.

Heinrich I wouldn't mind so much, except Golo's never written a book in his life.

Silence

Horváth If I were you, I wouldn't take any notice of all this, I'd just sit in my office and get on with my novel. You are writing a novel?

Heinrich Yes. I am. Is that what you do?

Horváth That's what I do.

Heinrich nods, digesting this advice. Horváth looks across at Helen. Silence

How did you get out of France?

Heinrich With extreme difficulty I think is the answer to that.

Pause

I had the papers for America and the Spanish visa and the Portuguese visa, but I couldn't get the French to give me an exit visa. Finally, there was this wonderful young American who said if I didn't go now, I'd be arrested and sent back to Germany. He took us to the Spanish border and we climbed out of France, over the Pyrenees.

Horváth How did you manage?

Heinrich I'll never know. I didn't mind the walking, but I kept falling over. If it hadn't been for Nelly, my wife, I'd still be there . . .

Pause. He looks at Horváth

You must meet Nelly, she doesn't get a chance to see many people her own age, all my friends are so ancient now.

Horváth I'd like to.

Heinrich I don't know how, but she managed to get us tickets on a Greek ship, she fought for them like a wild thing, the last Greek ship out of Europe before Mussolini invaded Greece.

Pause

Lisbon harbour, you know. I'm a continental European. I've never even been across the Channel. And the harbour. I can't tell you how beautiful it is. Like some long-lost love. To watch it vanish. Hard to bear.

Silence. His eyes are misty

My daughter's still there. With her mother, my first wife. I tried everything I knew, but I couldn't get them out of Prague.

Silence. Horváth struggles for a change of subject and finally hits on it

Horváth How is your brother?

Heinrich Tommy? He's bought some land out at Pacific Palisades. He's having a house built there.

Horváth He's all right, then?

Heinrich Well, his daughter's family was torpedoed a few weeks ago. She and the baby were rescued, thank God, but Tommy's son-in-law was drowned.

Silence. Helen gets up to leave. Despite the gravity of his expression, Horváth is unable to prevent himself from watching her as she goes

She catches his eye on the way out

How much are they paying you?

Horváth Hundred and twenty-five bucks a week.

Heinrich Me too. Yes. Me too.

Silence

I know what you're thinking, my boy. How is it we've managed to be so lucky?

Horváth rises to his feet, leaves his manuscript (from the previous scene) on the table, and moves downstage. Behind him, the Lights fade on Heinrich Mann

Horváth That wasn't at all what I was thinking. I was thinking that after the First World War, Heinrich was the most famous writer in Germany, when Thomas Mann was just a name. I remembered the rumours about their not being on speaking terms all through the twenties, and how in nineteen twenty-nine many of us believed the Nobel Prize had gone to the wrong brother. I was trying to control the sadness and anger I felt at rediscovering my old hero in some Burbank toilet.

SCENE 6

Salka Viertel's front room

Horváth By now, we émigrés had a favourite meeting place: a little house in Mabery Road, Santa Monica, which belonged to Garbo's writer, Salka Viertel.

The Lights come up slowly on the long table in the front room of the house; the table is set for dinner and lavishly decorated with flowers and candles. It runs diagonally across the stage and upstage of it is an opening which leads to the kitchen. Milling around, standing close to each other to suggest a confined space, are a number of guests, mostly of a certain age, formally dressed for the occasion; these include Salka Viertel herself, Thomas Mann, and his wife Katja, Lion Feuchtwanger, Walter the butler, and as many others as is feasible. Conspicuous among them, and somehow immediately obviously different from them, is a dazzling blonde woman: Nelly Mann. She's forty-three, and she's wearing a red silk blouse, stretching tight across her capacious bosom, and holding a glass of red wine, to which she has frequent recourse

We met here to celebrate Heinrich Mann's seventieth birthday; not actually on his birthday, because on that date Thomas Mann was receiving one of his honorary doctorates, this time at Berkeley. All the same, it was a notable occasion and one I would always remember, if only because it was there I first made the acquaintance of the famous Nelly.

By now, Nelly is at his elbow. She's somehow acquired a second glass of red wine which she holds out to him

Nelly Want some?
Horváth *(taking the glass)* Thank you.
Nelly It's the real French stuff, I think, God knows where she got hold of it.
Horváth Prost.

He takes a sip. Nelly takes a swig

Nelly Of course, I don't mind the Californian, what do you think?
Horváth I quite like it.
Nelly Yes, it's rough and strong, and what more do you need, I always say.

She laughs. Horváth smiles at her

All this lot are so bloody snobbish about it. What do you do?
Horváth I'm a writer.
Nelly You're not.
Horváth Yes. Ödön Horváth.
Nelly Bloody Hungarian, by the sound of it.
Horváth Well, you know, the usual Austro-Hungarian mixture.
Nelly I am disappointed. When I saw you over here, I said to myself, well at least I bet he's not a writer.
Horváth I'm sorry.
Nelly You don't look like a writer.
Horváth It's good of you to say so.
Nelly If anyone'd told me, when I was a young slip working the Kurfürstendamm, I'd finish up other end of the bloody world in bloody California with a lot of bloody writers, I'd have blacked his eye for him.

She turns, gesturing lavishly at the table. The others, meanwhile, are taking their places at the discreet urging of Salka and Walter

Heini doesn't want all this, you know. He's been dreading it for weeks. Who wants a lot of people telling you you're seventy? He knows he's seventy, poor old bugger. Bad enough turning forty, wouldn't you say?
Horváth Ah, there you have me.
Nelly Get off!
Horváth No, I promise you, it's a good few months yet.

Nelly snorts sceptically. Walter arrives alongside her, murmuring, sotto voce and gesturing at the table

Nelly All right. More wine, is there?

She sets off towards the table. Walter hurries to get a bottle of wine, then intercepts her and pours her another glass. Horváth stays where he is for a moment, watching her. The others are already placed around the table: in the centre, facing the audience, is Salka Viertel, Heinrich on her right and Thomas on her left. Nelly is opposite her, next to Lion Feuchtwanger and Marta Feuchtwanger is next to Heinrich

Horváth (*moving to the table*) I thought she was wonderful. (*He sits and turns to the audience*) After the soup and before the special roast beef she'd been saving, dear Salka Viertel, our hostess, rose to her feet. This proved to be a fatal error.

Salka is on her feet, tapping her glass to attract attention

Salka I just wanted to say what an honour it is for us to be holding this little celebration in our house and to propose a first toast to a great writer: to our beloved Heinrich Mann.

Everybody rises, except Heinrich. Into the ensuing minute pause comes Nelly's voice, clear as a bell

Nelly I need some more.

Silence. Feuchtwanger fills Nelly's glass. Then everyone raises his glass to toast Heinrich. Everyone sits. Salka turns and gestures to Walter. Walter turns and gestures to the kitchen

   Then, proudly, Toni Spuhler, the cook, emerges from the kitchen, bearing the roast

   However, as she does so, Thomas, his back to the kitchen, rises deliberately, fumbling for his glasses, which he then cautiously adjusts on his nose. Salka gestures to Walter. Walter in turn gestures to Toni who stops, transfixed. Thomas produces a substantial manuscript from the inside pocket of his dinner-jacket. Walter gestures again, more urgently

   Toni turns and retreats into the kitchen

Thomas clears his throat

Thomas This festive gathering then has finally taken place; and its cause—so moving and worthy a cause!—lies so far in the past, it is almost necessary to remind ourselves of it. The cause, my dear brother, is your seventieth birthday, which took place on March the twenty-seventh, and which we were unable to celebrate earlier. I was at fault for this, or rather my commitments were at fault ...

Horváth turns, as Thomas continues to deliver his speech

Horváth And on he went, as the beef sizzled and browned, to speak of Goethe and Nietzsche, of liberty and pragmatism and evil, till buttocks stiffened and eyelids drooped ...

The guests suddenly slump. Horváth turns back and Thomas's voice surges back

Thomas If genius, dear Heinrich, is foresight, the ability to anticipate, the passionate portrayal of things to come, then your work bears the stamp of genius. And if you have, as I'm sure you do, the organic stamina, your old eyes will see what you predicted in your youth: the fall of a tyrant.

He whips off his glasses: applause. He nods minimally in modest response; then sits. Salka gestures to Walter. Walter gestures to the kitchen. A few seconds pass and then:

   Toni with the roast beef

But, as she crosses the threshold, Heinrich rises to his feet. Toni freezes. Heinrich searches his pockets, momentarily at a loss. Desperate pantomime between Salka, Walter and Toni

   Finally, Toni, pale with rage, returns to the kitchen with the beef

Heinrich, meanwhile, has located his speech

Heinrich Thank you. (*Reading*) "Well, my dear brother, as you, in the course of your too kind address, so perceptively remarked ..."

Horváth turns to the audience, grinning and Heinrich's voice disappears

Horváth Afterwards, somebody explained to me they'd been doing this kind of thing ever since they were fifty. And so, at even greater length, as the beef shrivelled and blackened, Heinrich delivered his measured response.

The guests revert to slumped positions. Horváth turns back. Heinrich gives a little formal bow

Heinrich ... then, as indeed it is now. Thank you again. Nelly and I are profoundly grateful.

He sits, amid warm applause. Salka gestures to Walter. Walter signals to the kitchen

Presently, grim-faced, Toni emerges from the kitchen with the beef

She's hardly into the room, when Marta Feuchtwanger rises to her feet

Toni stops, staring in disbelief. Then she thrusts the beef into Walter's hands and, bursting into tears, rushes back into the kitchen. After a moment, Walter exits with the beef

Meanwhile, Marta, unaware of all this, has launched into her speech

Marta I should like to propose a toast to Nelly Mann, without whom I cannot think that this celebration would be taking place. Her cheerfulness and encouragement during that terrible journey over the Pyrenees will never be forgotten by any of us. So I would like to ask you ... (*She breaks off*)

Nelly has risen to her feet and now turns to face the audience, her back to the table. One hand is clenched across her breast, the other is covering her face. Her shoulders are shaking. Marta hurries round to her side and reaches up to pat her on the arm

I'm so sorry, I didn't mean to upset you.

Nelly Upset me? (*She breaks off, helpless with laughter. For a moment, she can't speak for laughing. She drops her hands and her blouse comes open, revealing a beautiful embroidered lacy bra*) No, Christ, I been laughing so hard, I've burst me button.

Peals of more uncontrollable laugher. Slight consternation among the guests. Salka rises to her feet to try to calm the situation

Black-out

Helen Schwartz's apartment

A spot comes up on Horváth

Horváth Well, I continued to work for the Warner Brothers, hoping that none of them would notice me, and sure enough, none of them did. And in the meantime, I found a new way, which was actually an old way, to improve my English.

Black-out. Pause

The Lights come up on Helen's apartment. Helen and Horváth lie entwined on the sofa. Silence

Helen Lot of American men don't like a girl to earn eight times their salary.

Horváth This is crazy. A girlfriend who takes me out to dinner and drives me to work, you want that I complain?

Helen European men must be different.

Horváth No. I think this er . . . Einstellung . . .

Helen Attitude?

Horváth Attitude, ja, is also common in Europe.

Helen Then it must be just you that's different.

Horváth I'm afraid yes.

Helen Actually, this is all highly irregular. As a rule, the two-thousand-dollar-a-week writers don't talk to the thousand-dollar-a-week writers, and the thousand-dollar-a-week writers stick pretty closely together.

Horváth So you are different also.

Helen It's just I'm a nice Jewish girl, I like to have someone to look after.

Horváth Yes, I have been once married to a Jewish girl.

Helen (*reacting*) Married?

Horváth Ja.

Helen You didn't tell me that.

Horváth Oh, it was just for the passport.

Helen What do you mean?

Horváth I married Maria to give her the Hungarian passport.

Helen Oh, I see. And what happened?

Horváth She used it and left. Gone with the wind.

Helen You been married many other times?

Horváth Oh, I think once is enough for anyone, don't you?

Helen I wouldn't know.

Horváth You know in the Fu Manchu movies, when he says, I can promise you a beautifully painful and slow, slow death? For me this is called marriage.

Helen I see.

She disengages from him gently, gets up and crosses the room to light a cigarette. Horváth sits up

Horváth Anyway, women have always been very kind to me.
Helen I don't know why that should be.
Horváth Me neither.

She smiles at him. Silence

What is it with these Warner Brothers? I write all these goddamn scenarios, no-one ever says a word to me.
Helen You want me to explain that?
Horváth Sure.
Helen It's what I was saying before.
Horváth What?
Helen First, they really don't like to read. So if they have to read, they're going to read what cost them money. Listen, their thirty-five-hundred-dollar-a-week writers earn more while they're taking a piss than you do all week. So whose scenarios do you think they're going to look at?
Horváth Yes, but I also am costing them money.
Helen That's peanuts, Ed. That's charity. You give a blind musician a dime, you don't expect the *Goldberg Variations*.
Horváth OK, but it's costing me time. Ten to five every day and the goddamn bus rides, when do I have time to write? My writing?
Helen You have a lot of time. You know why? Because no-one reads your scenarios. And actually it suits you that way, if the truth be known.
Horváth I suppose.
Helen So why are you complaining?
Horváth I like to be appreciated.
Helen You want them to pay you and appreciate you and shut up, right?
Horváth I think this is fair, yes. Like any artist.

They smile; then Helen looks away

I'm sorry. I know for you this is serious business.
Helen Yes, it is.

Pause

My folks took me to see *The Jazz Singer* in New York when I was fourteen. I thought it was terrible: God, so sentimental. But I was ... excited by it, you know? In those days I already knew I wanted to write, but I didn't know what.
Horváth And this decided you for the movies?
Helen No. It just started me thinking. A whole new medium. Infinite possibilities. Probably the first art form since Elizabethan theatre to appeal to every age group and every class. And you can take it out to audiences anywhere in the world. Now I can't imagine writing for anything but the cinema.
Horváth I understand you theoretic.
Helen I know it hasn't happened yet, I know the business is run by greedy opportunists and yes-men and chisellers, but they can't hold out forever. Just look at the progress that's been made in what, not even fifteen years.

Horváth Yes, but it's too powerful for them ever to listen to ze writers ...
Helen *The, th.*
Horváth Ach, zis goddamn sound. I know what is his answer, St Peter, when I come and say, OK, open ze gates: no, no, *the, the.*

She laughs, comes over and sits beside him again and takes his hand

Helen I liked your novels so much. I wish I could read your plays. Aren't any of them translated into English?
Horváth No, I'm sorry, I am not enough famous.
Helen What are they like, are they political, or what?
Horváth No, I think you wouldn't call them political, they don't deal about special ... Themen ...
Helen Issues?
Horváth No, and not from Marxist ideas, like Brecht.
Helen Who?
Horváth Bertolt Brecht, he's a writer, bit older than me. I just write about ordinary people, how bizarre they are. I write about life, as it regrettable is. I write about the poor, the ignorant, victims of society, women especially. The Left attack always: they say easy pessimism. But they love the people without knowing any people. I know the people, how terrible they are, and still I like them. Also, it turns out, my plays were not enough pessimistic.
Helen And what about the Right?
Horváth Oh, already, before ten years ...
Helen Ten years ago.
Horváth Ja, I was in court for fighting in a bar with Nazis. And when my play *Geschichten aus dem Wienerwald*, er, *Tales from Vienna Wood* was in Berlin premièred, the Nazi critic said, not even an audience of niggers would watch the play without they would protest. I stand by my review.
Helen Well, I wish I could read German. My father has family in Germany.
Horváth Oh? Where?
Helen Düsseldorf, I think. They're, you know, cousins. I never met them.
Horváth And are they still in Germany?
Helen Far as I know.

Deathly silence. Horváth shakes his head dubiously, then looks up and across at Helen, deciding to break the mood

Horváth You know something, you're the best-looking playwright I ever met.
Helen That's the kind of remark I usually take exception to.
Horváth Take exception, sorry?
Helen Don't like.
Horváth Oh. All the same, it's true.

Helen smiles at him

Helen You want to go out this evening?
Horváth No.

Helen What do you want to do this evening?

Horváth looks at her. Silence

Oh, so that's what you want to do this evening?

Horváth I think my English is getting better.

Helen gets up and moves away, looking back over her shoulder and smiling seductively. She leaves the room

Horváth, a slow smile spreading in anticipation, rises from the sofa and is about to follow her off, when all of a sudden the House Lights snap on, startling him considerably. He moves downstage, peering into the auditorium

SCENE 8

Advancing through the auditorium at a leisurely pace, inspecting the audience suspiciously, chewing a cheap cigar, is a slight, bespectacled man of forty-three, close-cropped, scruffy and unshaven, a scar on his left cheek, wearing a flat cap and a jacket with overlong sleeves and no lapels over an open-necked grey flannel shirt: Bertolt Brecht

Horváth Brecht always liked people to be aware that they were in a theatre. I said to him more than once, but Brecht, what makes you think they think they're anywhere else? But he had a way of not answering questions he didn't approve of.

By this time, Brecht has reached the stage, and the House Lights are off

Didn't you?

Brecht doesn't answer. Instead, as Horváth continues to speak, he approaches the set and inspects it, reaching up and rattling one of the flats, shaking his head in dismay

We'd met, of course, in Munich in the early twenties, but I never really got to know him, he always seemed wary of me; and I knew that although his teeth, unlike the shark's, were far from pearly-white, they were sharp enough to make it advisable to keep out of range of his jaws.

Brecht has found an apple in a fruit bowl on the set. He rubs it perfunctorily on his trousers and sinks his teeth into it. He takes his cap off and fans himself

He came direct from Vladivostok, ten days before the Nazis invaded Russia, just as the State Department was about to devise a really efficient way of keeping refugees out: they decided that no-one who had surviving close relatives in Germany should be admitted, on the grounds that they might be susceptible to pressure and let themselves be blackmailed into becoming Nazi spies. Consequently, he was one of the last émigrés to arrive.

Brecht Exiles.

His voice is metallic, slightly high-pitched, harsh. Horváth turns to him, surprised

Horváth What?
Brecht I don't like the word émigré. It somehow suggests I left of my own free will. I was driven out. I'm an exile.
Horváth Just as you like.
Brecht Look at this thing. Big and red and shiny and seductive and when you bite it tastes like an old sponge. Capitalist apples. (*He throws the apple away*)
Horváth We heard you were in Moscow.
Brecht Yes. But Moscow was no good, we couldn't stay in Moscow.
Horváth Why not?
Brecht I couldn't get enough sugar.
Horváth Did you have trouble getting out?
Brecht Money was the only problem. I had the visas, but I couldn't afford the tickets. Weigel, the children, my two associates, there were six of us, you see. In the end, I had to go to Feuchtwanger's publisher.
Horváth He gave you money?
Brecht Well, I said I was Feuchtwanger's representative, authorized by him to collect his royalties. Then I waved a letter from Feuchtwanger in his face. "How much would you like?" he said. "How much have you got?" I said.
Horváth And that was that?
Brecht Certainly. Feuchtwanger's very popular in Russia.
Horváth Did he mind?
Brecht No, why should he, he was delighted.
Horváth There was enough for all of you to get out?
Brecht Yes. We had to leave my ... Grete Steffin, she was ill, she had to go into hospital, she died.

Silence

You still do all your writing in bars?
Horváth I'm not choosy.
Brecht I heard that in Vienna you were always to be found in a café otherwise frequented entirely by dwarfs.
Horváth Yes.
Brecht You particularly interested in dwarfs or was it just affectation?
Horváth Well, you know something, I went to that place for years and in all that time I never met a Nazi midget.

Brecht smiles. Then he plucks at his jacket

Brecht It's so hot here, I can't stand this heat, you haven't any ice-cream, have you?
Horváth Sorry.
Brecht You should move out to Santa Monica, it's much cooler.
Horváth You're not on Argyle anymore?
Brecht No. Twenty-fifth Street.

Horváth That's a more appropriate address for you somehow.
Brecht The ice-cream is the only thing here I like.
Horváth You used to be so enthusiastic about America, all those plays you
wrote.
Brecht That was before I came here.
Horváth Doesn't say much for the revolution.

Brecht grunts, unsmiling

Brecht I wanted to ask you what it was like, working at the studio.
Horváth Boring. Time-consuming. Pointless.
Brecht I've heard it's better to work as a freelance and sell them stories.
Horváth If they'll buy them, yes, it is better.
Brecht Everything here is sell, sell, sell. At home, it's blood and soil and
racial purity, here it's sell. If they could, they'd sell their piss to the
urinal.
Horváth You got a car?
Brecht No.
Horváth Then it's no good working at the studio. Not coming in all the
way from Santa Monica.
Brecht That's what I thought.
Horváth I'll make some enquiries if you like.
Brecht No. I'll manage. I've always despised anyone whose brains can't
fill his belly.

Silence

Horváth Seen many people?
Brecht Well, I ran into Thomas Mann.
Horváth How was that?
Brecht Like stubbing your toe on three thousand years of history.

Silence

I've never felt so remote from the world, not even when I was stuck
away in the back end of Finland.
Horváth You really hate it.
Brecht I can't believe there is such a place and I don't know what the hell
I'm doing here. I used to read Shelley sometimes and think the poor
bastard's been dead a hundred years and all those injustices are still as
bad, if not worse, and then I'd think, will they be reading us in another
hundred years and feeling the same, and then I'd get depressed for a
while. But here I feel like that all the time.

Pause

Do you have any Lenin?
Horváth Lenin?
Brecht I didn't want any trouble with customs so I dropped mine over the
side at San Pedro.
Horváth The complete works of Lenin?
Brecht Yes.

Horváth At the bottom of the Los Angeles Harbour?

He smiles. Brecht is beginning to look annoyed

No, I don't have any Lenin.

Brecht I was afraid of that.

Brecht strides off through the auditorium

SCENE 9

Heinrich Mann's sitting-room

Horváth walks into the set to join Heinrich Mann, turning en route *to speak over his shoulder to the audience*

Horváth One autumn afternoon, Heinrich Mann and I came home early from the studio.

Silence. Heinrich shakes his head

Heinrich Now what?

Horváth Something'll turn up. Don't worry.

Heinrich I don't know, at my age ... What a profession it is. Not only is there no pension, but you're lucky if you get away before they kick your head in.

Horváth Wish there was something else I could do, but it's too late now, it's all I'm good for. It seems I was born to be a writer.

Outside there's a sudden screech of brakes and a muffled thud

Heinrich That'll be Nelly.

Horváth Would you like me to get you something? Just tell me where to find it.

Heinrich No, no, it's all right.

A moment passes and then Nelly enters, holding a glass of red wine. She's very surprised to see them

Nelly You're back early.

Horváth Didn't seem much point sitting out the last few hours.

Nelly No change, eh?

Heinrich No.

Nelly That bloody brother of yours.

Heinrich Tommy went personally to see Jack Warner ...

Nelly Oh, yeah, squeezed it in, did he, between trips to the White House?

Heinrich Nelly, he told me he pleaded with Jack Warner, it can't have been easy.

Nelly And what happened?

Heinrich He says Jack Warner laughed in his face.

Nelly (*pushing her wine abruptly at Horváth*) Here.

Horváth Erm.

Nelly Take it. We're not paupers, you know. Yet.

Horváth takes the wine

Nelly leaves the room briskly

Heinrich Strange thought, it's nearly fifty years since my first novel was published. Who could have imagined I'd end up being fired by Jack Warner?

As Horváth speaks, Nelly returns with a full glass, carrying the bottle in her other hand

Horváth We haven't been fired. It's just they're not renewing any of the European Film Fund contracts. It's an important distinction.
Nelly What, you mean like between eating earth and swallowing air?
Horváth Sort of.
Nelly So, what are we going to do?
Heinrich Well, move to a smaller house, I suppose.
Nelly We already moved to a smaller house.
Heinrich Even smaller.
Nelly Jesus.
Heinrich And I'm afraid the car will have to go.
Nelly Oh, no.
Heinrich Nelly ...
Nelly I can't be in this shit-hole without a car. Why d'you think I went to the trouble and expense of learning how to drive?
Heinrich There just isn't any choice.
Nelly (*to Horváth*) You know what, you know what he did this summer? They wanted to publish a book of his, American publisher, good money. They just asked him to make a few changes, that's all, one or two things they didn't like. So what does he do? He tells them to piss off.

Heinrich lowers his head, very unhappy, and shakes it slowly from side to side

Heinrich (*quietly*) I haven't worked all this time to make compromises.

Nelly looks at him: her expression softens

Nelly No, course you haven't, Heini, you're right, you're right, who the hell do these people think they are?

Heinrich looks up at her gratefully. She's smiling at him. They look at each other for a moment, then she turns away

Well, I can see how this story's going to end. (*Pause*) Back to work is what. (*She turns to Horváth*) Did you know, when Heini met me, I was a barmaid.
Horváth I had heard.
Nelly Oh, you had heard, had you, had you heard?
Horváth Yes.

*She looks at him fiercely for a moment, then relents, pours herself another
glass of wine and flops down on the sofa*

Nelly Quite soon after we met, Heini said to me, "Tell me about your life,
I want to know your life-story." "I'll do one better than that," I said,
"I'll write it out for you." So I did. So he reads it and he says, "This is
wonderful, I think I can do something with this." And I says, "Yeah, I
reckon I can do something with it an' all. I can have it published and
make a fortune." "That's as may be," he says, "but listen, just leave it
with me for a while." Well, he had it for months, I'd almost forgotten
I'd writ the bloody thing. Then one day he says, "You know that
manuscript you gave me", he says, "I've turned it into a novel." "Fine,"
I says, "you publish your novel and I'll publish me memoirs, and I'll
give you three to one I sell more copies." "Yes," he said, "that's what
I was afraid of, so I took the liberty of dropping your manuscript in the
stove." So don't talk to me about writers.
Horváth I wouldn't dream of it.
Heinrich It was very lively, Nelly's manuscript, but it was a little coarse-
grained.
Nelly That's why it would have been a bestseller, you silly old bugger,
then we wouldn't be in this dump.
Horváth You mean to tell me that's a true story?
Heinrich I never contradict a lady.
Nelly Never do what to a lady, don't you believe it. (*She chuckles, gets up
and crosses to Horváth, and pours him another drink*) Listen, I hear a
rumour you've taken up with some Jew.
Heinrich Nelly.
Nelly What's the matter, aren't we good enough for you?
Horváth I don't know what you mean.
Nelly Still, I suppose down there at the studio, that's probably all you
could find.
Heinrich Nelly!
Nelly Oh dear, spoken out of turn again.
Horváth I'm very pleased with the way things have turned out, thank you.
Nelly Well, that's all that counts. (*She moves easily back towards the sofa,
pouring herself another drink en route. She sits down, smiling pleasantly*)
So, Ödön, what are you going to do?
Horváth Well, I'm going to see Siodmak at Universal. He might have some-
thing, he's getting on quite well there. (*Pause*) So, if you need some help,
I'd be delighted, you know, a loan or whatever.
Heinrich My dear boy, it's very kind of you, we do appreciate it. But we
shall manage.
Horváth Well, please don't hesitate . . .

Silence

Nelly Tell you what, broke or not, we're giving you that fortieth birthday
party. Here.
Horváth Well, I . . .

Nelly I don't want any of that. I want, thank you, Nelly, how kind.
Horváth Thank you, Nelly.
Nelly And just to show all is forgiven, you can even bring your yid.
Horváth I don't know if she'll come, she's a bit particular about mixing with Germans.

Nelly looks at him for a moment, then grins suddenly. Horváth raises his glass

Here's to being unemployed.

They drink a toast. Horváth replaces his glass on the coffee-table and the Lights fade on Heinrich Mann's house

SCENE 10

Brecht's garden

As the toast is drunk and the Lights fade on the previous scene, Horváth moves downstage

During the following, Brecht enters, drawing a half-curtain in front of the Mann set. He is still puffing on a cigar and wearing his hat. He carries a square of green linen, which he arranges carefully on the forestage. When this is laid to his satisfaction, he produces, as if by magic, from his inside his jacket, a small sign, which he sets up behind the square. It says: brecht's garden

Horváth As winter drew in and the temperature fell to seventy, I received a postcard from Brecht. It was far from easy to decipher, since Brecht, somewhat literal-mindedly in my view, included punctuation in his crusade against capitalism, as if there were something imperialist about the very concept of a capital b. Anyway, the gist of it was that I was summoned to an audience in Santa Monica.

He goes over to join Brecht, who, in the meantime, has sat down on his garden

Brecht How are you managing?
Horváth Carefully. I'm getting eighteen dollars fifty a week unemployment pay.
Brecht Wonders of the welfare state.

Horváth sits down on the ground, nodding wryly

I thought you might like to write a film with me.
Horváth Oh?
Brecht I'm working on three or four at the moment. With different people. With two of you, you can bang one out in a week. My theory is, if you bombard the studios with stories, they're bound to accept one sooner or later.
Horváth What sort of stories?

Brecht Give you an example, I'm working on one with Thoeren, do you know him?

Horváth No.

Brecht He's very successful, works for MGM.

Horváth A girl I know, American, asked me the other day what *Ars Gratia Artis* meant over the gates at MGM. I told her it meant "abandon hope all ye who enter here".

Brecht Well, you're right, Thoeren is impossible. He's all over the place. He hasn't the first idea as to plot. He keeps saying, "Now as I see it, there are three possibilities—he can ask for money *or* he can sacrifice his life for the cause *or* he can make his mother pregnant." It's like working with a chicken with no head. On the other hand, he makes a fortune.

Horváth And what's the story?

Brecht It's a romantic comedy. American and a Portuguese are planning a huge business deal, which they must keep secret from the competition, so they write to each other in code, in the form of passionate love letters. American censor, girl, reads the letters, gets fascinated. Then she meets the man, who falls for her and pursues her, without knowing she knows he's writing those letters. Endless complications. Happy ending. It's a piece of shit. Ingrid Bergman would be great.

Horváth Why?

Brecht Because she's wonderful.

Horváth What are you calling it?

Brecht *Bermuda Troubles.*

Silence

What I mean is, it should be possible for you and me to put our heads together, scientifically, and come up with something just as good as these mindless hacks.

Horváth Yes, in theory. Just as bad, you mean.

Brecht Doesn't have to be bad. I'm doing a better one for Charles Boyer. With Kortner.

Horváth Oh, how's he?

Brecht Vitriolic as ever. I like working with him. I made him angry yesterday. He's been doing the research and he found out that in the nineteenth century in the Mediterranean seaports, the whores would sometimes have to take on more than a hundred customers a day. He was very shocked. Finally I said, "You bloody liberals are all the same: 'A hundred a day! What inhumanity! Eighty at the most!'"

Horváth (*smiling*) He's a good actor.

Brecht Very. But there's no work for him here.

Horváth Why not? Peter Lorre works all the time.

Brecht Yes, sinking slowly into the quicksand, grinning from ear to ear.

Silence

Horváth Whatever happened to Carola Neher?

Brecht Neher?

Horváth Didn't she go to Moscow?
Brecht Yes, with her husband, yes.
Horváth I adored her.
Brecht Did you?
Horváth Rumour was, she was your mistress, when she was in *The Three-penny Opera.*
Brecht Was it?
Horváth Did you see her when you were in Moscow?
Brecht She was arrested a couple of years ago. They both were.
Horváth What for?
Brecht Ostensibly for Trotskyist activities in Prague.
Horváth That's ridiculous.
Brecht She was always very naïve.
Horváth And what's happened to her?

Silence. Brecht shakes his head

Brecht Far as I know, she's dead.
Horváth How appalling.
Brecht The innocent, you know. (*Pause*) I think they deserve everything they get.

Long silence. Then Horváth rises and moves downstage. As he speaks, Brecht picks up his garden and sign and starts to move off. Horváth touches Brecht's arm and indicates the half-curtain, as if to say it's no good to him. Brecht shakes his head pityingly and removes the curtain, revealing Heinrich Mann's sitting-room

Brecht exits

Horváth It was good of him to ask me to collaborate with him. It was his way of expressing concern. But even as I agreed to think it over, I knew we would never be able to work together.

SCENE 11

Heinrich Mann's sitting-room

A spot comes up on Horváth

Horváth The following weekend the Japanese attacked Pearl Harbor. We show folk knew where our duty lay and we were not slow to retaliate: all performances of *Madame Butterfly* at the Met were cancelled and the Greenwich Village Savoyards withdrew *The Mikado* from their repertoire. All the Japanese gardeners in Hollywood were fired. In the case of an air raid, *Variety* advised its readers to seek shelter in the Nora Bayes Theatre, on the grounds that it had never had a hit. So: on Sunday, Pearl Harbor. Monday, war was declared. And on Tuesday, I was forty. I've known better starts to the week.

The Lights come up on Heinrich Mann's sitting-room

Nelly, festively dressed, enters with a tray of glasses and an open bottle of wine. She puts the tray down, looks around, quickly pours herself a glass, drinks, and replaces the glass. Then, as Horváth continues to speak, the room gradually fills with the personnel from Salka Viertel's party (including Heinrich, Thomas and Katja Mann and Lion Feuchtwanger), with the addition of Brecht and Helene Weigel, his gaunt, hollow-cheeked wife. Meanwhile, Nelly whispers something to Heinrich, and makes her way out to the kitchen

I phoned Nelly to ask her if the party was still on. "Why shouldn't it be?" she said. It was nine o'clock in the morning. She was drunk.

Helen Schwartz enters and collects two glasses of wine. She joins Horváth as he comes to the end of his observations

Helen came by to collect me and drive me over. She was a little late, perhaps because she was nervous about meeting all those formidable Germans.

Helen hands him a glass of wine and together they join the fringes of a group being addressed by Thomas Mann

Thomas I'm simply unable to understand what it is they do to their writers here. It happens time and again. They write one good book, then two mediocre ones and that's the end of their career. They have no conception of a developing life-work. No stamina. They get drowned in success.
Helen (*to Horváth*) What's he saying?
Horváth (*in English*) He says there are no American writers.
Helen (*turning to Thomas*) Oh? What about Fitzgerald, Hemingway, Faulkner, Dos Passos, Steinbeck, Nathanael West?
Thomas (*in English*) I did not mean to wound your sensibilities, Miss Schwartz. I can only speak as my old-fashioned eyes discover.

Heinrich comes over to Horváth

Horváth Where's Nelly?
Heinrich In the kitchen, I believe, preparing something for you.
Horváth Shall I go and ... ?
Heinrich No, no, I think she wants to surprise you.
Brecht (*to Thomas*) I can't agree with you either. If you want a writer with real inventiveness and staying power, what about Erle Stanley Gardner?
Thomas I'm afraid I am not familiar with his work.
Brecht Well, he's not Simenon, of course, but he's about the best they have over here.
Thomas I'm obliged for the advice. (*He turns back into his group*)

Brecht moves off with Weigel

Brecht (*muttering to her*) I can't understand what he's saying half the time, his mouth is full of money.
Heinrich Well, the English seem to have got off to a pretty poor start in Libya. After all that build-up.

Weigel What's the world coming to, when Churchill is our only hope?

Brecht It doesn't matter how modern their weapons are, I'd say in the hands of the oldest and most corrupt aristocracy in the world, they are bound to misfire.

Horváth Oh, really, I thought shooting was the one thing the English aristocracy was good at.

Heinrich They don't have the spirit of the Russians. Did you see that thing about the fighting in Rostov? They're attacking the Panzer troops with frying-pans.

Brecht The Nazis have condemned them for illegal methods.

Heinrich That's right, tanks are allowed but frying-pans are illegal.

Brecht All this stuff about the Japanese is all over the front pages, but I found something inside the *LA Times* yesterday I think is much more significant. The German advance on Moscow has broken down because of sub-zero temperatures. So, on the day the greatest industrial power in the world enters the war, it's finally dawned on Hitler that in Russia the winters are cold. He's finished. The house-painter is finished.

Horváth (*turning to Thomas*) The Americans will declare war on Germany as well, won't they?

Thomas Oh, yes, before the end of the week, I think I can guarantee that.

Suddenly, the assembled company is silenced by a raucous sound from the kitchen: Nelly's voice yelling out; "Happy Birthday to you ..." Everyone turns to look at the kitchen door

Nelly appears. Sensation. She's carrying a birthday cake with the candles lit. She's naked

Nelly sings "Happy Birthday" to Horváth, then hands him the cake, which he takes uncertainly from her. Silence

Nelly Well, blow out the candles, aren't you going to blow out the candles?

Horváth does so, as best he can

Now you have to make a wish. (*Coquettishly*) Can you think of a wish?

Silence. Nelly turns away from Horváth to include everyone

Well, I've had to sell all my jewellery, every last piece, so I thought, what the hell, why wear anything? (*She turns on Thomas*) Hello, maestro, you've never seen your sister-in-law like this, have you? Now what do you think of me? (*She moves towards him*)

Thomas (*turning away*) Control yourself.

Nelly That's all you can say, isn't it? That's all you can think.

Heinrich (*gently*) Nelly.

She turns and stares at Heinrich for a few seconds. Then she turns back to Horváth

Nelly If you knew what it's like to be married to such an old, old man. He's so old. He's so old.

She bursts into tears. Horváth slips off his jacket and wraps her in it
He clasps Nelly to him, covering her face, then leads her slowly off
Nobody moves. Tableau

*Horváth reappears, in his shirtsleeves, and passes through the guests, taking
no notice of them. As he speaks, the Lights go down on them and they
silently disperse*

Horváth It's true to say that none of us was really happy. But as I expect
you've noticed by now, I saw things differently from the others. You
see, I had always loved what was strange and half-finished. I loved
gullibility, cheap religious mementos, plastic, superstitions, pornography
with spelling mistakes, girls dressed as mermaids, streets without end,
the ethics of the fairground, the bright smiles of the no-hopers, motive-
less friendliness, the pleasures of nomads'-land. In short, after two years
in Los Angeles, I knew I was home.

He strolls off

The House Lights come up

ACT II
1942–50
SCENE 1

Light show: garish neon. Franz Waxman's music for Sunset Boulevard.
Projections: Hollywood landmarks of the forties

Horváth steps into this, grinning

Horváth Ah, Hollywood! The kitsch! The *désespoir!* (*He watches the projections for a moment*) The pagodas! The *châteaux!* The mauve haciendas! Donuts! Dentistry! Divorce!

Everything snaps off. Total darkness

The black-out.

Pause

Right, that's quite enough of that.

The Lights come up on a corner of The Sleeping Beauty, *a dingy bar on Hollywood Boulevard. Hal, the huge, jovial barman, is behind the bar. There's a table for one covered with papers: among them a glass of red wine. Not far off is another table where Angel sits, nursing a scotch on the rocks. Horváth glances at all this, then turns back to the audience*

Well, I got by. Siodmak did what he could and before too long I had my first credit, shared with only four others, for a really sleazy horrorpic, not to be confused with Garbo's latest, called *Two-Headed Woman*. In Germany, I'd always used a pseudonym for my film work, but here that seemed like an unnecessary vanity. I had said goodbye to the theatre. I had no reputation to guard anymore. I moved smoothly along to the next piece of work, which had to do with the adventures of a barbershop quartet. (*Pause*) I had my routine now. I had a room with a Murphy bed in an apartment building north of Hollywood Boulevard. I'd stroll down the hill, buy a paper on the corner of Hollywood and Wilcox from a charming dwarf called Angelo, have breakfast in the local drugstore, coffee, juice, toast and one egg over easy, then I'd wander past the Crossroads of the World to Sunset and Highland and take a bus across the hills to Universal City. I appreciated the way that even when you were down and out, the place names did their best to make you feel important. (*Pause*) All I needed now was some little haven conducive to work and contemplation; and before long I discovered the ideal spot. (*He gestures at the set*) The Sleeping Beauty Cocktail Bar on Hollywood Boulevard. (*He goes and sits down at his table, sips at the wine*) I even taught Hal, the barman, how to make a Glühwein, hot red wine with cinammon. It's hardly the climate for it, but it did make Hal's wine a little more palatable and every sip was molten nostalgia.

Brecht appears and spends a moment peering irritatedly round the dimly-lit bar. Then he gestures up at the lighting-box

Immediately the stage is saturated in hard white light. Horváth looks up, blinking crossly

There's no need for all that, you know.
Brecht Force of habit.

Horváth waves to the lighting-box and the lighting returns to normal

Horváth Welcome to the office. What are you drinking?
Brecht I don't know.
Horváth Glühwein?
Brecht Christ, no, what a horrible idea.

He draws a chair over to Horváth's table and sits. Horváth, meanwhile, calls over his shoulder in English

Horváth Hal? Glass of iced water for my friend.

Brecht contemplates the table for a moment, his expression severe

Brecht How can you work in such chaos?
Horváth I know where everything is.
Brecht I need order.

Horváth nods as if Brecht has stated the obvious. Hal comes over to the table with a glass of iced water in his great hand. He puts it down in front of Brecht

Hal Big spender, huh, Ed? (*He wipes the table down*)
Brecht What did he say?

Horváth shrugs, diplomatically feigning incomprehension. Then he hands his empty glass to Hal, frowning at him in mock disapproval

Hal More of this shit?
Horváth If you please.

Hal goes back to the bar to prepare the drink. Brecht watches him go with distaste

Horváth How's work?
Brecht Same as ever. Hollywood roulette. At the moment I'm writing a picture for Lorre.
Horváth What about?
Brecht He plays an actor, émigré ...
Horváth Émigré?
Brecht Yes, in London, completely broke, gets taken up by a millionaire banker with a palazzo in Berkeley Square.
Horváth Yes.

Brecht Everything's fine until he falls foul of the butler, Sniffkins ... Oh, forget it.

Silence

Horváth Sniffkins?

Brecht Well ...

Horváth Yes.

Hal brings Horváth's Glühwein and then goes back to the bar

Brecht I really hate it here.

Horváth (*looking around*) It's not so bad, better than my room.

Brecht I don't mean this dump. I mean the whole poxy, godforsaken city.

Horváth Oh, I see.

Brecht I don't know what I can do here, I feel like a sausage in a greenhouse.

Horváth I'm just beginning to enjoy it.

Brecht It's pretty, all right, the ocean, the hills, the lemon groves. But if you look more closely you'll see every one of those damn trees has a price tag on it. That's the way it is everywhere here. What have you got? Let's have a look! Deliver the goods! And everything with a smile, all this ... depraved cuteness.

Horváth I don't mind that.

Brecht And you know what the worst thing is? When you take your place in the line with all the other whores and pimps and pushers, there's one thing you feel more than anything else, and it's what really makes me ill, and what it is is hope.

Horváth It's certainly a good deal more common than charity or faith.

Brecht Shelley said that Hell must be like London, ha, what did he know?

Silence

By the way, I found out what it is they do, all those people at the studios.

Horváth What?

Brecht They all have different jobs, you see. One has to check the consistency, another one the quantity, somebody else makes sure it's brown and someone else again tests it for smell. Finally, they get together, all these specialists, and compare notes. Only then do they let themselves get excited: It is! It really is! It's genuine cover-to-cover shit! Let's shoot it!

Horváth And of course, once they shoot it, it's dead.

Brecht Yes; and I also found out the secret of being a successful screenwriter.

Horváth Tell me.

Brecht You have to write badly, you have to write very, very badly, *but you also have to write as well as you possibly can.*

Pause while Horváth works this out. Then he smiles broadly

Anyway, what the hell's the use of a medium that can't react to its audience?

Horváth All the same, you're still trying.
Brecht Unsolved is not the same as insoluble.
Horváth Well, that didn't come out of a fortune cookie.
Brecht It's depressing, though. The other day I was working on some rewrites in a play and something which hardly ever happens: I got stuck. And for the first time, suddenly, I had a glimpse of what it must be like to be untalented.

Silence

Horváth Was there something special you wanted to see me about?
Brecht Heinrich Mann.
Horváth What about him?
Brecht He's starving to death.
Horváth Surely not.
Brecht Literally.
Horváth I thought Thomas sent him a cheque every month.
Brecht He sends some measly amount. Last month it didn't arrive. So, not only no groceries, but his teeth were hurting and he couldn't go back to the dentist, because he owes him.
Horváth I gave Nelly some money last time I saw her.
Brecht You mustn't do that. She just drinks it.
Horváth I don't care what she does with it.
Brecht Well, it doesn't get to him is what I'm trying to say.
Horváth All right, I can give you a hundred. But you're going to have to wait till the end of the week.
Brecht OK. Thanks. Thanks.
Horváth I can't believe Thomas is allowing this to happen.
Brecht What does he care? He basks up there in the Palisades, like some old lizard, wallowing in money, with his secretary and his servants and his five cars and his brother's down here, sweating and broke, with an insane wife and not even enough to get his shoes repaired. It's like an image of everything that's most depressing about our profession. Heinrich saw the way things were going before the last war, he understood about Fascism, while Hitler was still slapping paint on beer-halls. Thomas thought that war was just what Dr Nietzsche ordered, he supported it, he thought democracy was some new-fangled French fad that wouldn't last ten minutes in Germany.
Horváth But he changed his mind.
Brecht That's exactly what I mean. Any opinion he holds today is an opinion he opposed five years ago. He's been rewarded for having been as slow-witted and impotent as his bourgeois public. And Heinrich's been punished because he was right all along.
Horváth Literature has to do with more than being right.
Brecht Literature? His books can be of no benefit to anyone. Except possibly weight-lifters. But that's not what I'm talking about. Did you know Hitler was in power three years before Thomas Mann could bring himself to say a word against him? That's what I'm talking about.
Horváth I can't condemn him for that.

Brecht Well, I can. And I do. And you should.

Silence

Horváth I'll give you the money on Saturday. Anonymously, if you don't mind.

Brecht I don't mind. (*He looks at his watch*) I guess it's time we were going.

Horváth We?

Brecht The curfew.

Horváth Oh.

Brecht I suppose we're lucky they haven't put us in camps like the Japanese.

Horváth What's this us?

Brecht Us Germans.

Horváth I'm a Hungarian.

Brecht frowns, puzzled. Horváth smiles blandly. Brecht rises to his feet, looking slightly annoyed. He stretches out his hand. A perfunctory handshake

Brecht Goodbye.

Horváth Goodbye.

Brecht leaves

Hiatus. Horváth shuffles one or two of his papers idly. Then he looks up and catches the eye of Angel at the next table. She smiles at him. Brief silence

Angel Mind if I join you?

Horváth Please.

She gets up, carrying her glass, and crosses to his table

Hal!

She sits. Hal appears. Horváth gestures at her glass

Ordinary red wine this time for me.

Hal Ordinary's what it is. (*He goes to the bar*)

Horváth smiles at Angel

Angel Thought your friend was never going to go.

Horváth Me too.

Hal brings the drinks

Horváth What's your name?

Angel Just call me Angel.

Horváth You're an actress.

Angel How did you know?

Horváth smiles

Maybe you've seen me in something.

Horváth Maybe.

Angel I had a swell scene in *West Point Widow*. But they cut it.
Horváth Shame.
Angel And I was in *Destry Rides Again*. In all the saloon scenes.
Horváth And here you are again. Cheers.

They drink

Angel He was getting pretty excited, your friend.
Horváth He does.
Angel I thought maybe you was spies.
Horváth (*mock-indignation*) Spies? I'm a Hungarian.
Angel Gee.
Horváth No, I am no spy. But I am an enemy alien. This means I have to be indoors by eight o'clock. Curfew.
Angel Oh.
Horváth So we will have to continue our discussions at my place.

He rises to his feet and gathers up his papers. Angel looks up at him, a touch hesitant

Angel You got a car?
Horváth I only live just up the hill.
Angel What do you do?
Horváth I work at Universal, same as you.

Silence. Then she gets up, smiling, and takes his arm. They stroll out of the bar together, favoured by a sardonic grin from Hal

Hal goes to the table, clears the glasses and returns to the bar as the Lights fade briefly

SCENE 2

The Lights come up on The Sleeping Beauty

Hal is still behind the bar washing glasses. He looks up as Horváth strolls in on his own and goes towards his table. He carries his papers

Hal Hi, Ed.
Horváth Red wine, I think, tonight.
Hal No, it's too hot for that. What you want is a nice Chablis.
Horváth I need your opinion, I send you a postcard.

Hal enjoys this. By this time, Horváth is at his table, stirring his mess of papers

Hal vanishes offstage

Horváth concentrates on his papers for a moment. From outside, the screech of brakes

After a time, Nelly Mann makes an uncertain entrance, peering around the bar

Horváth looks up and sees her before she ses him

(*Getting up and going to her*) Nelly.

*She blinks at him and smiles unsteadily. He shakes her hand. Then he leads
her back to his table*

Hal!

Hal (*off*) Yeah? Now what?
Horváth Bring the bottle. (*He helps Nelly into a seat*) How are you?
Nelly Fine. I'm fine.
Horváth And Heinrich?
Nelly Oh, he's fine.

Hal arrives with an opened bottle of red wine and two glases

Hal Shall I pour it out or do I leave it to breathe?
Horváth Go shit in your hat.
Hal That's good! (*To Nelly*) He's improving. (*To Horváth*) I'm proud of
you.

*He goes back to the bar, glancing at Nelly, who hasn't reacted at all. Horváth
pours a glass of wine for her. She drinks it off, fast. He pours her another*

Horváth I heard things had been a bit difficult.
Nelly Yes. It was sweet of you to give us money.
Horváth Who told you? I ...
Nelly Nobody. I guessed.

Silence

Horváth Brecht said ...
Nelly Yes, that was all a bit of an exaggeration. Tommy's cheque went
astray in the post. He was away. Panic. When he came back he wrote
another cheque and paid off all Heini's debts. He's not a bad old sod.
Except him and Heini's not on speaking terms any more.
Horváth Why not?
Nelly Oh, it's my fault, I suppose. (*She pours herself another glass of wine,
as she does throughout the rest of the scene*) He came around to read us
another great chunk of that terrible old *Joseph* crap. I was in the kitchen
and I was just singing to myself, you know, to cut out the drone, when
he suddenly says, very loud: "Is that the dog?" Is that the dog, I ask
you? We haven't got a bloody dog. So I says: "No, it's me." And he
shouts in: "I know you've never had a very high opinion of my work
..." "I don't know," I said, "anyone who can write the line: 'Like all
the Krögers, she looked distinguished', has to have some talent."
Horváth I don't understand.
Nelly Kröger, it's me maiden name. Nelly Kröger. Fine old German name.
Horváth Oh, I see.
Nelly Anyway, he perks up a bit and says: "I never knew you were an
admirer of *Buddenbrooks*." "I don't know about admirer," I said, "but
the first four pages were ever so good."

Silence. She drinks

It's not him, really, he's all right; it's his wife. Jewish cow.

Horváth Nelly, do stop.

Nelly You know what he said to Heini, when he came back from his first date with her? He said: "You know, she's not a bit like a Jew."

Horváth Really?

Nelly Shows how much he knew. I don't know, there's him and there's you and there's Brecht, what's so special about them?

Horváth I don't want to talk about it, Nelly.

Nelly Where's yours, then?

Horváth In New York.

Nelly Oh, and when the cat's away?

Horváth We try not to think in those terms.

Nelly You know what, you can be a real pompous bastard when you put your mind to it.

Horváth looks hurt

Come on, cheer up.

Silence

Horváth So you're all right for money now?

Nelly Yes. Tommy does what he can for us. He's not as rich as everybody thinks he is. Heini told him to keep the Nobel Prize money in Switzerland, lots of people did, but he wouldn't listen and the Nazis took the lot. They stole his house and the SA Commandant in Munich is driving his car.

Pause

I got a job, what about that, then? In a hospital.

Horváth Nursing?

Nelly Washing sheets.

Silence. She drinks

Yes, that's right, it's awful. But at least I've been able to buy a car. On credit.

Horváth Is it worth it?

Nelly Course it is. Also I did something clever. Really dozy bitch handling the sale, so I gave my name as Kröger. That way if there's any problems with the car, I can just sell it and get another one.

Horváth You can't be serious.

Nelly Why not? They'd never find me. I even gave them a false address. Brecht's. (*She chuckles*)

Horváth shakes his head wonderingly

Horváth You'll get in terrible trouble.

Nelly I been in trouble all me life. That's one of the reasons I hate this place, it's so boring.

Horváth (*looking at his watch*) I'm sorry to say this, Nelly, but I think it's time we were going. The curfew . . .

Nelly There's no curfew for you. You're a bleeding Hungarian.

Horváth I know, but there is for you.

Nelly Well, why don't you let me worry about that?

Horváth Let me take you home.

Nelly I didn't know you could drive.

Horváth Anyone can drive.

Silence

Nelly I could always spend the night at your place.

She stares boldly across the table at him. Horváth looks back at her, confused but tempted

Horváth That's right, you could . . . (*He breaks off and reflects for a moment*) What about Heinrich?

Nelly He doesn't mind.

Horváth Of course he minds.

Nelly Listen, how would you know, he's not your bloody husband, you don't have to live with him.

Horváth I have to live with myself.

Nelly I don't need all these bloody excuses, if you don't fancy it, just say.

Horváth It really isn't that at all.

Silence

Nelly I'm so lonely. (*Pause*) Do you want me to say please?

Pause

   Please.

Horváth sits there, torn. Nelly puts a hand over her eyes and starts sobbing silently. Horváth reaches over to touch her arm

Horváth I'll take you home.

She pulls away from him

Nelly I'm not going anywhere near that squalid dump tonight.

Horváth Well, then, I'll take you wherever you want to go.

Nelly I'll take myself.

She's on her feet, takes two steps away from the table, then turns back, grabs the wine bottle, turns away again and hurries out

Horváth watches her go, then sits for a moment, pondering. Then he looks up at the audience

Horváth I didn't normally allow conscience or sentiment to influence me in these matters. Indeed, I lost my virginity in Budapest with a nice married woman, whose husband was away at the front. It was just the image of that old man sitting alone in that tiny house on South Swall Drive, waiting.

Horváth exits
The Lights fade

SCENE 3

The beach. A clear winter's day
The Lights come up on Horváth and Helen strolling along a deserted beach,
arm-in-arm. Roar of the surf

Helen When I was back East, somebody gave me some transcripts of the
speeches Thomas Mann's been making for the BBC.
Horváth Yes.
Helen He says they've been taking Jews out of Holland and sending them
to be gassed.
Horváth Yes, this is easily possible.
Helen But if they're doing that, what can they be doing to the Jews *in*
Germany?

Horváth hesitates before answering

Horváth I don't know, but if you imagine the worst you can imagine,
probably it will be worse.
Helen But what's happening? I'm a member of the Anti-Nazi League, but
nobody's told us about these things. Why don't we know more about
it? Why doesn't somebody do something?
Horváth What can anyone do?
Helen I think just standing by and letting it happen is as bad as taking
part in it.
Horváth Well ... (*He looks away*)

She stops, releases his arm and stands still, looking at him. He comes to a
ragged halt, still avoiding her eye

Helen Don't you care about it?
Horváth Of course I care about it. From the beginning I have been writing
about how Germany is. Perhaps I am not enough a good writer. In any
case, no-one has listened. What can I say about history? People like to
watch accidents.
Helen Sometimes I think you're very cold.
Horváth Yes. Well, yes.

Silence

Helen Well, I need at least to feel I'm trying to do something, even if it's
an illusion. I've decided to join the Party.
Horváth The Communist Party?
Helen Yes.

Horváth shrugs, his expression dubious

You disapprove?

Horváth I can't take these people seriously. Here in America, the far Left, compared to the Left in Europe, they're like Republicans. Every other kind of extremism you have but you don't seem to have the talent for political extremism.

Helen I'm not interested in extremism, I'm interested in getting things done: opening the Second Front, repealing the Smith Act, helping to organize the migrant workers.

Horváth All this is fine. I just don't like to join.

Helen No commitments, uh?

Horváth Yes, maybe.

Helen Feel the same about politics as you do about people?

Horváth I like to keep ... freedom of action, yes. Also, I have very bad experiences with joinings. All kinds.

Helen So you've given up. Too old, right?

Horváth I think a writer must be always outside. You tell better the truth from standing looking in the window than from sitting at the table.

Helen Yes, but why should you have to stand on your own?

Horváth hesitates a moment before deciding to confront the question

Horváth Why do you ask me these questions? You know how important is maintaining independence. For your work also.

Helen I know, but with you there's no choice.

Horváth If this was wrong for you, we would not still be friends after years.

Helen I wasn't talking about us anyway. I was talking about taking a stand.

Horváth Is the same thing, you see. In America, everything is personal. So if I smile at the Communist Party, it is because for me is like a game, a luxury you can afford if you have too much compassion in the bank. In Europe is life or death.

Helen That doesn't entitle you to be patronizing.

Horváth I know this, and I don't mean it, but I also know what you have to do in Europe just to get through the day. And I left in 'thirty-eight, before the real horrors started. Even so, there are things in my conscience you would never believe.

Helen I expect I might be able to guess.

Horváth No. Never. (*He stands for a moment, looking out to sea*)

Helen Soon be warm enough to swim.

Horváth Not for me, not here. This goddamn sea is too big. I need a human scale and a flat water.

Helen Why is it, when it comes to anything really large, you're afraid to let yourself go?

Silence. Instead of answering, Horváth begins to stroll along the beach again. Helen lets him go a few paces, then follows

Horváth You know what, I am starting to write a play.

Helen Really? (*She catches up with him, pleased, and takes his arm*)

Horváth That's right. First time in five years.

Helen But that's wonderful.

Horváth makes a wry grimace

Isn't it?

Horváth I don't know. It hurts. Like learning to walk on a broken leg. But it will give me something to do evenings when you are at the, you know, meetings.

Helen almost bridles, then decides not to take offence. They stroll off, arm-in-arm

The Lights fade

SCENE 4

Heinrich Mann's sitting-room

Music: the orchestral version of Friedrich Holländer's "Und Sonst Gar Nichts" ("Falling in Love Again") from The Blue Angel

The Lights come up on Heinrich Mann, sitting alone, as imagined by Horváth in his small sitting-room, staring at the wall

The doorbell rings. Heinrich doesn't stir. The doorbell rings again. This time he registers it and slowly rises to his feet. The music fades as he crosses to the door and lets Horváth in. They shake hands, and Heinrich gives a small formal bow. Forming the background to this scene, the occasional sounds of passing traffic. Heinrich shows Horváth to the chair he has been sitting in

Heinrich It's very good of you to come so promptly.

Horváth It's a pleasure.

Heinrich I know what it is, getting about in this town.

Horváth What can I do for you?

Heinrich It's Nelly.

Horváth Oh?

Heinrich I'm very worried about her. And I know she thinks a great deal of you, so I was hoping you might be able to ... help her.

Horváth In what way?

Heinrich I may as well come to the point. She seems to have got herself into trouble. She ran into a parked car and she was arrested. Thank God, for some reason, they failed to notice she was drunk, but she's on some kind of reckless driving charge and there's also, I mean I don't understand the ins and outs of it, this is the second car she's had just recently, and there seems to be some kind of irregularity in the paperwork. She's always been very careless about that kind of thing, and what with the language difficulties ... Anyway, she's in despair about it. She's convinced they'll send her to prison.

Pause

I just thought maybe you could help to reassure her. Make her see sense.

Horváth Well, I'll do whatever I can ... where is she?

Heinrich I don't know. She said she was going to work, but I'm sure she hasn't been in all week.

Horváth Well, suppose I start by finding a pay phone and calling the hospital?

Heinrich That's very sensible, but I've already done that myself.

Horváth I see.

Heinrich I thought perhaps you might have some idea of where she might spend her time. I don't really know, you see, how well you know her.

Horváth Well, I, well, no.

The doorbell rings. Heinrich looks up surprised, and goes across to open the door

After a few murmured words, he lets in a saturnine, fortyish figure: Jacob Lomakhin, the Soviet consul from San Francisco. He speaks with a heavy Russian accent

Heinrich leads him into the room

Heinrich Ödön, Ödön von Horváth, this is Jacob ...

Lomakhin Jacob Mironovich Lomakhin, at your service.

Heinrich Herr Lomakhin is down on a visit from San Francisco. What can I get for you? No vodka, I'm afraid, but I think there may be some wine in the house.

Lomakhin No, no thank you, Herr Mann, in fact, perhaps I call back later, my business is rather confidential.

Heinrich Herr von Horváth is a respected colleague. I have no secrets from him. (*To Horváth*) Herr Lomakhin is the Soviet consul.

Horváth Perhaps it's time I was on my way ...

Heinrich No, no, I insist.

All this has happened very quickly and now there is an awkward silence

Lomakhin Very well. (*He reaches into his inside pocket, brings out two large bundles of banknotes, and slaps them down on the table*) On behalf of Soviet government, it gives me greatest pleasure, Herr Mann, to make presentation of some monies against your Russian-language royalties.

Heinrich I don't know what to say.

Lomakhin These represent small fraction of what is owing. You see your books have sold more than half million copies in Soviet Union.

Heinrich No.

Lomakhin So, as I say, should be more, but I hope you will find these acceptable.

Heinrich I'm overwhelmed, when your nation is in the midst of such a bitter struggle, that you should——

Lomakhin (*holding up a hand, interrupting him*) Please, please. Is great honour for me. (*He turns to Horváth with a charming smile*) Herr von——?

Horváth Horváth.

Lomakhin You are also writer.

Horváth Plays mostly.

Lomakhin I stand open to correction, but I don't believe your work is performed in Soviet Union.

Horváth Heigh ho.

Lomakhin Yes.

At this moment, there's the sound of a key in the door and Nelly appears. She freezes on the threshold

Nelly Is this the police?

Heinrich (*hurrying over to her*) No, no, no. This is Ödön and this gentleman is the Soviet Consul. Herr Lomakhin, my wife, Nelly.

Lomakhin bows deeply. Nelly stares at him suspiciously, as Heinrich closes the door behind her

Lomakhin (*kissing her hand*) Enchanté.

Nelly (*turning to Heinrich*) What's he want?

Heinrich He's brought us some money. My Russian royalties.

Nelly What?

Heinrich indicates the money. She stares at it incredulously

My God.

She rushes impulsively over to Lomakhin and kisses him on both cheeks. He takes a step back, startled

That's for Stalingrad.

Lomakhin Thank you.

Nelly It's a miracle, what you people are doing.

Lomakhin We think, when we break through, it will be turning point of war.

Nelly God knows last year was the saddest year of my life, and this one's been even worse, but the way you Russians have kept your end up ... it's been an inspiration to us all.

Horváth has been watching her, slightly taken aback by this outburst; Lomakhin, on the other hand, is delighted

Lomakhin You're very kind. I appreciate.

Nelly No, no, it's us. We appreciate. Have a drink.

Lomakhin Thank you, Frau Mann, but no. I have some other business to attend to ...

Nelly Go on, be a devil.

Lomakhin No, really. I am so pleased. Good-afternoon.

Heinrich I'll show you to your car.

Lomakhin No, no, thank you. I am usually followed by FBI boys. Today, I think I have given them slip, as we say in America, but to be on safe side, I park two, three blocks away. I would not wish to give you embarrassment. So I say good-morning.

He shakes hands with them. General salutations

Lomakhin leaves

Nelly picks up one of the bundles of money

Nelly How much?

Heinrich Later, dear, we have a visitor.

Nelly Well, so we do. Long time no see, how are you, Ödön, don't answer that, back in a minute.

Nelly drops the money and vanishes into the kitchen

Horváth looks at Heinrich

Horváth She's high as a kite.

Nelly returns from the kitchen with a glass of red wine

Nelly So, Heini tell you what's happened?

Horváth Yes.

Nelly And aren't you going to say, I told you so?

Horváth No, I'm not.

Nelly Then what are you going to say?

Horváth I don't know, I . . . Your husband says you're very worried about this whole business.

Nelly Wouldn't you be?

Horváth Is there anything . . . I mean, do you have a lawyer?

Nelly (*pleasantly*) Listen, why don't you piss off and let us count our money?

Heinrich Nelly, really.

Horváth No, no, she's quite right. I'm afraid I can't be much help.

He turns and moves abruptly downstage. The Lights dim on Heinrich and Nelly

That night Nelly took an overdose of sleeping pills. She was rushed to hospital and her stomach was pumped. She wasn't fit to appear in court. Heinrich did his best to smooth things over. She was sent for a spell to Camarillo State Hospital.

SCENE 5

Salka Viertel's front room

A spot on Horváth downstage

Horváth In the New Year, all kinds of things began to improve. First, to begin at the bottom, my career. There was, for a brief moment, a vogue for anti-Nazi films. Brecht, for example, had written one for Fritz Lang. And now Siodmak managed to persuade someone at Universal that my novel, about which we had had our original meeting all those years ago in Paris, would make a good film. So, I was able to move into a two-room apartment, buy a pre-war black Studebaker (fortunately, as my driving methods were individual, a sturdy vehicle) and, most important of all, work on a screenplay with other than a mechanical professionalism. But all of this, of course, was completely insignificant compared to the tremendous excitement of knowing that the tide had finally turned against Hitler. The prospect of peace, needless to say, immediately unleashed a series of bitter quarrels among the émigrés.

The Lights come up on Salka Viertel's front room, less festively arrayed, of course, than it was for Heinrich Mann's birthday. Present are Heinrich and Thomas Mann, Brecht, Feuchtwanger and three or four others, all men. A discussion is raging. Horváth watches a moment, his expression glum. He goes reluctantly over to join the others

Thomas I still think the opening is a shade abrupt. Couldn't we agree on some appropriate preamble? Just to explain who we are.

Brecht Anyone who reads the letter will know who we are.

Thomas I don't so much mean who we are as what we are.

Brecht Isn't the fact of the matter this business about mentioning the Soviet Union?

Thomas Certainly, I don't think it's altogether prudent to talk about the Soviet Union in the opening clause of the letter. The Americans won't like it, you know. Do we have to refer to Russia at all?

Brecht sighs audibly

Brecht We've already discussed all this *ad nauseam*. How can we respond to an initiative coming out of the Soviet Union without saying that's what we're doing?

Thomas I don't want you to get the impression I'm at all hostile to Russia. On the contrary, I made a record to be distributed, to the Red Army, congratulating them on their noble victories.

Brecht I expect they'd have preferred you singing "Lili Marlene".

Thomas Shall we return to the matter in hand?

Brecht All right, if you want to write another sentence, write another sentence and we'll consider it.

Silence

Heinrich What I don't think much of is the business about "the Hitler régime and those elements favourable to it". That's a bit clumsy, isn't it? A bit vague?

Brecht "Classes" would be better than "elements".

Thomas looks up sharply from his piece of paper

Thomas Oh, really, do you think so?

Heinrich Why don't we come right out and say what we mean? The Hitler régime and the *corporations*?

Thomas I don't think that would be at all advisable. When the Vice-President introduced my speech at Madison Square Gardens, he made it quite clear that any criticism of——

Heinrich All right, all right.

Thomas We're visitors in this country, Heinrich. It's only polite to be circumspect.

Brecht (*muttering*) God help us.
Thomas What about "the Hitler régime and its criminal supporters"?
Heinrich Oh, go on, finish your sentence.

Silence

Horváth Couldn't we fetch the ladies?
Brecht Why?
Horváth They'd be able to wrap this up in ten minutes.

Silence

Thomas (*looking up*) Now. I don't see how anyone could object to this.
(*Reading*) "At a moment when the Allied victory approaches, we, the
undersigned German writers——"
Horváth German?
Brecht Writers?

Pause. Thomas frowns

Thomas "We the undersigned German-speaking writers, scientists and
artists consider it our duty to make the following public statement."
How's that?
Brecht Wonderful.
Thomas Any objections?

Silence

I feel that softens the hammer-blow of the opening, don't you?

Silence

Well, Horváth, as you're so anxious to fetch the ladies, please do, and
we'll try it out on them.

Horváth leaves the room

Heinrich You know what I think, Tommy? I think we have laboured
mightily and brought forth a mouse.

Thomas frowns but replies imperturbably

Thomas Mice have their uses.

*Horváth returns with Nelly and Katja Mann, Helene Weigel, Salka Viertel
and Marta Feuchtwanger*

*There are murmured greetings. Thomas clears his throat, stands and picks
up his piece of paper. Silence*

"At a moment——"

He's interrupted by a hoot of laughter from Nelly. He looks at her, pained

Nelly (*pointing at the piece of paper*) That all you come up with in four
hours, Jesus, Mary and Joseph, call yourselves writers?
Thomas Nelly, please.

She controls herself with some difficulty. Silence falls. Thomas clears his throat and starts again

"At a moment when the Allied victory approaches . . ."

Horváth slips away downstage as Thomas's voice fades away and the Lights dim to a spot on Horváth

Horváth Well, I'd had enough, quite enough, more than enough, so I took the opportunity, as he read, to melt away. I was passing through Westwood Village before it dawned on me that I'd forgotten to sign the letter . . .

SCENE 6

Horváth's sitting-room

A spot on Horváth downstage

Horváth I was scarcely out of bed the next morning when there was an insistent pounding on my front door.

Insistent pounding. The Lights come up on Horváth's modest sitting-room. He crosses it, sighing with some annoyance, to open the front door

Brecht enters. Without saying anything, he advances into the room, unfurling a large banner, which he displays prominently and which stays in place throughout the scene. It says: TWO FELLOW-DRAMATISTS REACH THE PARTING OF THE WAYS

Horváth considers the banner dubiously for a moment, then turns to look questioningly at Brecht

Brecht You'll never guess what that old reptile's done.
Horváth What old reptile?
Brecht He phoned Feuchtwanger this morning and withdrew his signature.
Horváth Do you mean Thomas Mann?
Brecht You call a meeting because you want to say something like this: Hitler is not the same as Germany and we call on our comrades there to rise up against him. Fine. Except the meeting is dominated by some pernickety old maiden-aunt who fiddles about with it for hours until it says: It's our view or at any rate the view of most of us or at least the view of enough of us to make it perhaps worth stating that Hitler is *not necessarily* identical in every respect with the rest of the German people and we think it would be awfully nice if they could devise some way of making this clear to the rest of the world, preferably without giving offence, and providing of course they make absolutely sure no Commies are involved. Then he calls up the next morning and says, that letter, oh dear, I think that was pitching it a bit strong, you'd better take my name off it.

Horváth Did he give any reason?

Brecht Apparently Roosevelt has some crazy idea that in a putative postwar capitalist Germany, Thomas Mann would make an ideal President. Of course, he keeps modestly declining, like some simpering geriatric virgin, but the fact of the matter is he doesn't dare offend the State Department. (*He sits*) Also he says it's too soon to declare our support for the German people when we don't know what horrors may be uncovered in the future.

Horváth That seems to me a fair point.

Brecht Oh, really, it seems to me equivocating crap.

Horváth It's not as straightforward as all that, this business about the German people: after all, they did vote for Hitler in pretty considerable numbers.

Brecht Well, you know I don't altogether approve of elections.

Horváth That's another matter.

Brecht No, the only thing that makes me suspicious about the Germans is that for thirty years, and without being compelled to do so by twenty divisions of the SS, so many of them obstinately persisted in reading the works of Thomas Mann.

Horváth There's nothing wrong with Thomas Mann. Except that he believes his reviews.

Brecht And you sneaked off without signing the damn thing at all.

Horváth Coffee?

Brecht Sure.

Horváth fetches a cup and pours coffee as Brecht lights a cigar. Brecht gets up and collects the coffee and ladles in quantities of sugar

Horváth (*grimacing*) How can you smoke those evil things?

Brecht These? They're El Capitan Corona. I have them sent from New York.

Horváth You mean you smoke them by choice?

Brecht Oh yes, for me, these are the means of production.

Horváth You're doing better now at least, aren't you? I saw your Lang film. Some good things in it.

Brecht It was shit. They screwed me.

Horváth How?

Brecht First of all it was misery working with Lang. Misery. Every suggestion I made he said: "They won't buy that. That they won't buy." Sometimes he said: "Yes, they'll buy that." Finally I said, "Listen, I know in this country they keep artists in cells padded with money, but do you have to remind me of that every time you open your mouth?" Then they cheated me on the credit. It was my film even though they fucked it up. I took it to arbitration at the Screenwriters' Guild. I worked with that bastard Wexley every day for ten weeks and at the hearing he came on as if we'd hardly ever met. You know what, just being in the same room with all those moral cripples, I could taste the vomit at the back of my nostrils. And to top it all off, they underpaid me.

Horváth But you did make some money?
Brecht Yeah. Bought some new trousers.
Horváth And a Buick.
Brecht Yes, with a rumble seat.

Silence

What happened to your film with Siodmak?
Horváth We missed the wave. Apparently they've stopped making anti-Nazi films. So Siodmak's doing *Son of Dracula*.
Brecht See what I mean? Not that the theatre's any better here. It's all part of the same great emotions racket.
Horváth I don't know anyone in the theatre.
Brecht The way it works, it's so naked. Somebody gets an idea, Ben Hecht, say, and then he goes round personally to all the investors and explains it to them. And they say: "Great, Ben, put me down for a thousand dollars." Can you imagine? If you talk to anyone about a theatre collective, they look at you as if you just escaped from Camarillo.
Horváth I heard a good definition of a theatre collective the other day: a theatre collective is a group of actors and technicians who, after frank, exhaustive and democratic discussion of any given topic, will then decide to do exactly what Brecht wants.
Brecht Oh, yes, who said that?
Horváth Can't remember.
Brecht Well, let's face it, when it comes to directing, there's Chaplin and there's me.

Silence. Brecht takes a piece of paper out of his inside pocket

Now. What about this signature?

He hands the piece of paper to Horváth, who looks at it for a moment

Horváth I genuinely forgot to sign last night. I just wanted to get out of there. But now I look at it ... No-one's interested in what I think about all this: *I'm* not even interested in what I think about it.

He hands the piece of paper back to Brecht

Brecht So you're chickening out as well.
Horváth No. I just can't see the point of it. It seems meaningless and self-important.
Brecht To do nothing is as bad as to be on their side.
Horváth I know that. And I've done far worse things than not sign this bit of paper. But that's my business, isn't it?
Brecht Well, I must say this confirms my worst fears about you. Now I know why, even though you're a talented man, your work is so detestable.
Horváth Oh?
Brecht It's this disgusting passivity. You people don't understand that in the theatre it's not enough just to interpret the world any more: you have to change it.

Horváth I really think you underestimate people's intelligence. They don't want blueprints, they don't want instructions. They're being told what to do all day: they don't want to come into a theatre and be told what to do all over again. They want to be told what they are.

Brecht That's the easy way out.

Horváth No, it's not, lies are what's easy. The truth is invariably difficult.

Brecht Don't start throwing metaphysics at me. This isn't the country for metaphysics. This is the funeral-parlour of the spirit. You know what I'm doing here to keep myself sane? I'm preparing a version of the Communist Manifesto in hexameters. Just to be in touch with some pure reason in this hell-hole, where everyone's tongue is brown and you have to be a freak to be normal.

Horváth I've never understood why a love of mankind in general should so often be accompanied by a profound dislike of the individual. Any theories? Besides, I've always been fond of freaks. Listen, you've been there, I've always wondered, what happens to transvestites in the Soviet Union?

Brecht I must say, this is shaping up to be one of the most eccentric defences of capitalism I've ever encountered. You're asking for a land fit for transvestites?

Horváth Yes.

Brecht I see.

Horváth After all, civilization depends, does it not, on our awareness of the sufferings of others.

Brecht Civilization? No, that's three kinds of fork and four kinds of wine. It's a device for maintaining the bourgeoisie's sense of superiority.

Horváth No, that's snobbery, that's something different.

Brecht Listen, I have people to see, I can't stand here all day quibbling over vocabulary.

Horváth It's probably best if we agree to respect our differences.

Brecht Well, that's the most boring suggestion I've heard all week. You can respect my differences if you like. I despise yours.

Horváth I see, you like to win arguments.

Brecht I did, didn't I? There's certainly no point coming second.

Horváth Well, that's the American way.

Brecht I'm off.

He turns and starts moving towards the door. Horváth points to the banner

Horváth Do take that thing with you.

Without a word, Brecht pulls down the banner, bundles it up in his arms and goes

Well, that was the last I saw of him.

He moves downstage and the Lights fade on his apartment

SCENE 7

Heinrich Mann's sitting-room

The Lights come up on Nelly and Heinrich. She is slumped in an armchair and looks terrible. He looks old and exhausted. Horváth joins them and takes a seat. They sit in silence for a moment

Heinrich I don't know, I'm at my wits' end.

Horváth I'm not quite clear, what exactly happened?

Heinrich She, well, you know, she ... her licence ...

Nelly I'll tell him, shall I, as long as I'm in the room.

Heinrich All right.

Nelly I was going mad here. There was someone I needed to see. Last week I went out and hired a car and drove over. On the way back I had a head-on collision at a junction. It was entirely my fault. They tested me and said I was drunk. I was. Also there was a case of wine on the back seat. Trial's on Monday.

Horváth Oh, Christ.

Nelly They're going to send me to jail, I know it.

Horváth No.

Nelly What do you know?

Horváth I'm sure they won't.

Nelly It's like a jail already, this place. For me, the whole city's like a bloody great open prison. How'm I going to stand a real jail?

Horváth You mustn't jump to conclusions, Nelly.

Heinrich That's what I keep telling her. You mustn't jump to conclusions.

Nelly This conclusion jumped to me.

Horváth Now, look, we just have to put our heads together. I'm sure there's all kinds of things we can do.

Heinrich Of course there are, any number of things.

Nelly Don't keep repeating everything he says like a parrot, Heini, you're giving me a headache.

Heinrich Don't forget, my brother has the ear of the President.

Nelly I took a lover, Ödön, he's very young.

Heinrich Excuse me.

He rises stiffly and leaves the room

Nelly scarcely notices his departure

Nelly I should never have come here, never. They all treat me like dirt, every one of them. Except for you, Ödön. And Heini, of course. They think I'm not good enough for him.

Horváth I'm sure that's not true.

Nelly I was never really happy anywhere except Berlin. I didn't care what anyone did, it didn't make any difference to me, none. I just fixed the drinks and decided if I felt like it tonight. I should never have left.

Horváth Why did you?

Nelly I never met anyone who was kind to me like Heini was. I suddenly

got it into my head that was the most important thing and I just went
away to find him.

Horváth I'm sure you were right.

Nelly No. No, because kindness isn't the only thing, Ödön. It's not ...
everything, is it, sometimes it isn't enough.

Horváth I know what you mean.

Nelly I can't do without that boy ... even though ... and, you know, I'd
take any ... you know what I'm saying ... it's not that.

Horváth Yes.

Nelly Any ... humiliation.

Horváth Don't.

Nelly But nothing touches ...

Horváth Yes.

Nelly ... his brutality or his indifference.

Horváth Don't let it, you shouldn't, find someone else.

Nelly There was a time, you know, when everybody, everybody wanted
me ...

Horváth I'm sure.

Nelly (*stretching out her hand to him*) Help.

*He takes her hand. Silence. The Lights dim. After a time he lets go of her
hand, rises and moves downstage. A spot follows him*

Horváth I couldn't. Nobody could. Before I left, Heinrich told me he'd
disposed of all her sleeping pills. But she fooled him.

*As he speaks, Nelly makes her way over to Heinrich's desk. She pours herself
a glass of water from the carafe, then opens a drawer and brings out a bottle
of pills. She starts taking handfuls of them, moving quickly. When she finishes, she drops the bottle into the wastepaper basket and lies down, curling
up on the stage in the foetal position*

And so the whole weary scene was played again. But this time with a
difference.

As he continues, Heinrich comes back into the room

*He rushes over to Nelly and drops to one knee beside her. Then, as Horváth's
story moves towards its climax, strobe lighting. In its harsh glare, Heinrich
can be seen grappling with Nelly's body, heaving it up and struggling across
the room with it, as if in some appalling dance*

He bundled her into a taxi and got her to the nearest hospital. But they
were very busy, as it was just before Christmas, and they didn't like the
look of this shabby old foreigner, who didn't have enough money on
him, and they refused to take his cheque. So he had to call another taxi
and set off to another hospital, where they were regretfully forced to
take the same attitude, but at least told him of a third hospital, where
he might expect better luck. He'd kept the taxi waiting this time just in
case, so they were able to speed off without delay to hospital number

three, where indeed they were far more helpful and were able to tell him right away that Nelly had just died.

The strobe cuts out

Heinrich and Nelly vanish

The spot isolates Horváth

A few weeks before, I had been to a fund-raising meeting for Roosevelt in Bel Air. Thomas Mann, who was now an American citizen, spoke. He appeared sandwiched between a conjuror who told an interminable story about a Chinese called Rosenthal and a lady ventriloquist; and was marginally less well received than either. All the same, you could tell that America had taken him to its heart. And from then on, whenever I thought about America, the two images, one seen and one imagined, rose before me: Thomas, on that white podium in that manicured garden; and Heinrich, weeping and covered with vomit, pleading with the admissions clerk in some casualty department, trying to get some attention paid to his dying wife.

Silence

SCENE 8

Horváth Well. The war was over. (*He looks up*) We lost.

Pause

And those of us who by chance had not been murdered had to consider whether or not we should go home and try to make our peace with those who, by chance, had not murdered us. Most of us drifted into staying. By now, I had worked 'my way to the top of the hill, to a small pink stucco rancho-style cabana. I even had a minute swimming pool or waterhole, in which it was necessary to swim in circles. Also, I still loved America. Despite everything, I was still devoted to its tragic innocence. However, the wave of post-war optimism which buoyed us up was soon to break. All over Hollywood, supporters of liberal causes, of the War effort and of our glorious Ally began to discover, often to their own amazement, that they were in fact premature anti-Fascists, fifth columnists, Red stooges, subversives, or even (*he whispers the word*) Communists!

Over this last sentence, "America the Beautiful" plays; however, within two bars it segues disconcertingly into the "Internationale". Horváth grins wolfishly

Opportunists crawled out of the woodwork! Buffoonish sub-committees proliferated! Idealists went to the wall! Nixon was invented! (*Quieter*) And my taste for the bizarre and ridiculous was gratified to the full.

The music stops

Naturally, one of the first to be summoned before the House UnAmerican Activities Committee was ...

A spot on Brecht, wreathed in cigar smoke

Bertolt Brecht.

Here the questions are from the recording of the actual hearing on 30th October, 1947

Voice of Robert E. Stripling Mr Brecht, did you ever make application to join the Communist Party?
Brecht Er, I do not understand, er ... the quest ... er, the question. Did I make...?
Voice of Robert E. Stripling Have you ever made application to join the Communist Party of any country?
Brecht (*interrupting*) No, no, no, no, no, no, never.

The spot on Brecht snaps out

Horváth Well, that fooled them. The following day, he left America for good, flew back to Europe and entered into his kingdom. Thomas Mann was also to feel hounded out eventually by McCarthyite stupidities; he chose to return to Switzerland where he could supervise the destiny of European culture from an appropriate height. As for Heinrich, he was invited back to East Germany to be President of the German Academy of Arts. I wanted to say goodbye to him so I drove out to Santa Monica, to the tiny apartment they'd found for him after Nelly died. I found him in the grip of a singular delusion.

SCENE 9

Heinrich Mann's bed-sitting-room

The Lights come up on the small bed-sitting-room. Heinrich, who's now seventy-eight, has aged shockingly since we last saw him. Still, he seems in good enough spirits. Horváth joins him

Heinrich Of course, the position is largely honorary, but there will be a great many official duties. I'm rather dreading that side of it.
Horváth I'm sure it won't be that bad.
Heinrich Still, it's not a thing one turns down: to be President of East Germany.
Horváth I thought ...

He cuts himself off, as Heinrich turns to him

Heinrich They wanted me to stand in the nineteen thirty-two elections, you know, against Hitler and Hindenburg. I refused. I didn't think writers had any business meddling in politics. I was wrong ... so this time I really must take up the challenge.
Horváth Yes, I see that.

Heinrich They tell me I'm a millionaire now. Only in East German marks,
but still. Nice to die a millionaire.
Horváth Yes.
Heinrich Only thing that worries me is having to work with Ulbricht.
Awful servile little creep. You'd be sitting around a table with him and
all of a sudden he'd announce it wasn't a table, it was a duckpond. And
the little bugger wouldn't let you go home until you finally agreed that
yes, looked at from a certain angle, you had to admit it was very like a
duckpond.
Horváth Now he's Party Chairman.
Heinrich He'll be completely unbearable.

They smile. Then a shadow crosses Heinrich's face

I've been getting those émigré dreams again.
Horváth Oh, what are yours?
Heinrich You know, waking up in Berlin, being recognized, arrested,
dragged off ...
Horváth Mine are always Vienna: can't speak the language any more,
pocketsful of American money, can't remember where anything is ...
Heinrich I'm frightened about going back.
Horváth That's understandable.
Heinrich I told you about my wife, my first wife and daughter?
Horváth Yes ...
Heinrich They put them in a concentration camp, you know. Just for
being my wife and daughter, no other reason.
Horváth I know.
Heinrich Mimi died soon after they let them out, but my daughter ...
those years, all those years in Theresienstadt, what am I going to say to
her when I see her?

Silence

Horváth I'm sure she couldn't possibly blame you.
Heinrich How was it we were so lucky? Something else I keep seeing in
my dreams, all those queues, all those queues of desperate people outside
the Consulates in Marseilles. Waiting all day and then turned away.
Why didn't that happen to us? I mean, what's so special about writers?
Horváth I don't know. I don't know.

Silence

Heinrich All the people I've loved most, you know, life was too hard for
all of them. Both my sisters, Nelly, my nephew Klaus, they all killed
themselves. Why do you suppose that is?

Horváth is groping for an answer. Heinrich goes on without waiting

Most extraordinary thing, did I ever tell you? When my sister Carla
died. At the time she was the person who meant most to me in the
world. I was out walking in the Tyrol, when I suddenly heard her calling
out to me, clear as a bell. Heinrich, Heinrich. When I got back to the

hotel, there was a telegram. She'd taken enough cyanide to kill a company of soldiers. I know I heard her voice. Hard to believe, but I promise you it's true.

Horváth No, I find it very easy to believe.

Heinrich Since then seems my whole life has been like that. To hear people crying out from distant countries. And nothing I could do about it.

Silence

I think Nelly would have been all right if she'd stayed in Europe. But she couldn't of course; she was frightened they'd find out she was Jewish.

Horváth What?

Heinrich Oh, yes, Kröger, he was only her stepfather. Real father was a man called Noa Troplowitz. Galician Jew.

Silence. Horváth shakes his head, amazed. Very quietly, the music: "Und Sonst Gar Nichts"

I'd left her, we'd said goodbye, she was a lovely, painful memory. I was working in my study in Bandol-sur-mer, the afternoon sun on my desk, when I heard a sound behind me, in the room. I turned round and she was there. She'd got out through Denmark, then all the way down to France. Saved all the money out of, I don't know, tips. And I wasn't a young man, then. It's the most beautiful thing anyone's ever done for me.

He stops talking, staring ahead of him. After a moment, Horváth rises and moves downstage

Horváth He talked to me about her for an hour or so and then I left. I felt a dull ache as if I'd lost something I'd never owned.

As Horváth continues to talk, Heinrich gets up and crosses to a large wardrobe, which he opens. It's full of women's clothes. He runs a hand along them, pausing every now and then. Finally, he selects Nelly's red blouse. He takes it over to the bed and lays it out gently. Then he kneels by the bed and buries his face in the blouse. Eventually, he's still, his arms outstretched, his cheek against the blouse, his eyes unfocused

He never got back to Europe. A couple of weeks later he spent an evening listening to Puccini—divine Puccini—went to bed and never woke up.

The Lights fade to a follow spot on Horváth

Thomas Mann's son-in-law called the thirties "a low dishonest decade"; but the fifties, which we were now embarked upon, looked worse. Black-listing, far from being, as I had supposed, a passing phenomenon, became institutionalized; and our American colleagues began to be faced with the same choices which had tormented us in Europe before the war.

SCENE 10

Helen Schwartz's apartment

As Horváth finishes speaking, Helen Schwartz wanders disconsolately into the circle of light. Horváth puts his arm around her

The Lights come up on Helen's apartment. Horváth leads Helen gently into the room. She looks shattered and confused. She's formally dressed: a suit and hat. Horváth busies himself fixing her a large scotch and ice. She looks around as if uncertain whether to sit down; finally she takes off her hat and throws it down on a chair. Horváth hands her the drink and she takes a big slug. A moment's silence, except for the clink of ice caused by the trembling of her hand

Horváth All over.

Helen Yes, you said it.

She takes another swallow of scotch

Horváth Aren't you relieved?

Helen I guess so. But all those days and nights preparing myself and getting more and more terrified, and then to be in and out in two minutes. As long as they're going to destroy your career, I'd've thought the least they could do was put a little effort into it. It's kind of insulting when they make it so obvious how insignificant they think you are.

Horváth It's not that. It's just they are bored with people taking the Fifth. You heard the others. "I refuse to answer this question on the ground it might incriminate me." They don't want to listen to this all day.

Helen Then they ought to mind their own fucking business.

Horváth Sure. Of course.

Silence. Helen sits down. She puts her glass down. Finally she speaks in a small flat voice

Helen I'm never going to work again.

Horváth kneels in front of her and takes her in his arms. Tears start to roll down her face, but she makes no sound

Horváth Of course you are.

Helen No. Listen, Twentieth didn't even wait to see how it turned out. Soon as they heard I got a subpoena, they fired me.

Horváth They must have known you weren't going to name names.

Helen Jesus, how could anyone do that? How could they?

Horváth To keep the pool, the maid, the subscription to the golf club, the wife.

Helen But to inform on your friends. Jesus.

He kisses her

Horváth I admire so much what you did. So brave. (*He gets up and paces around for a moment*) What are you going to do now?

Helen I don't know.
Horváth Are you going to go back East?
Helen Why? (*Pause. She looks at him*) You're all I've got now.

He looks away. Long silence

Horváth What you did today. I ... (*He breaks off*)
Helen Yes?
Horváth I compare it with myself and ...
Helen What do you mean?
Horváth Listen, there is something, all this time, I never told you.
Helen (*looking at him*) Don't.
Horváth (*nodding gravely*) Yes, I must. (*He takes a deep breath*) In nineteen thirty-four I joined the German Writers' Union.
Helen Well, I don't see what ... (*She breaks off; her expression changes*) In nineteen thirty-four?
Horváth That's right. I should say the Nazi Writers' Union.
Helen I ... don't understand. Why?
Horváth If you wanted to get work or to be published, you had to join.
Helen Oh, I see.
Horváth No, because it was not only this. I had to swear an oath that not even one of my grandparents was Jewish. I had to be certified ... politically unobjectionable.
Helen You don't have to tell me all this.
Horváth No, I must get this right, it was more than this. I had to find witnesses, what you call them, references, to say I was politically reliable. One I asked was this old cretin professor who had written a book: *Adolf Hitler, Progress Through Will-Power*. He signed. He said I was ... most suitable.

Silence

So, my boot also was on your people's faces.

Long silence

Only thing I can say in my defence, I never paid the dues.

Neither of them smiles

I was in two and a half years before they threw me out, and in all that time, nothing I wrote was worth shit.
Helen I don't understand how you could want to do that?
Horváth Did you read *Death in Venice*?
Helen Yes, of course.
Horváth It was a little like this, I could not leave the plague-infested city. But it was not beauty and innocence which kept me ... enthralled, it was the grotesque, the triumph of stupidity, the ugliness.

Silence

But, no, there are no excuses.

Pause

I should have told you before.

Helen shakes her head

Years, since years this has been a stone in my heart.

Helen gets up and moves uncertainly around the room for a moment. Then she goes over, sits next to Horváth and takes hold of his arm

Helen It won't make any difference.

Horváth It will.

She shakes her head again and kisses him. He holds her close for a moment

Yes it will.

Slowly he detaches himself from her and moves downstage as the Lights fade on Helen

It did. A month later she left for New York but she'd already travelled further away from me than the width of a continent.

SCENE 11

A poolside in the garden of a Bel Air mansion

A spot on Horváth downstage

Horváth For me, now, Los Angeles had become a city of ghosts: and I was suddenly aware that, just as before, I was standing by and watching the poison spread. Also, I found I was starting my thirteenth year in Hollywood; and I've always been a prey to superstition. And I wanted to work in the theatre again; by now I had four unperformed plays in my desk drawer. However. As I was making the arrangements to go back to Europe, I was offered a job. Nothing very interesting of course, just the sequel to a dull but surprisingly successful comedy called *Bedtime for Bonzo*—but I thought it might be better to go back home with a full pocket rather than a half-empty one. Just to be on the safe side, I consulted Dieterle's astrologer. He swore by her. When I put the situation to her, she became extremely agitated. I must take the job, she said. Otherwise I would miss the greatest experience of my life. Well, I'd heard all that before, but I never could resist it. The day of the meeting I got up early. The dawn chorus was on strike, except for a single warbling blackleg. The smog, a wartime innovation, hung low this morning, in snot-green stripes across the valley. My old Studebaker had broken down again, so I summoned a taxi to take me to Bel Air. I arrived late.

The Lights come up on the poolside in the garden of a Bel Air mansion. Art Nicely sits waiting in a canvas chair, an expression of well-bred impatience on his patrician features. He's about fifty, tanned, slim and manicured, tight

grey curls, T-shirt and bathing shorts. He gets up as Horváth comes stumping
towards him across the lawn. They shake hands. He waves Horváth to a chair.
Horváth sits, takes his hat off and drops it on the ground

Sorry I'm late.

Nicely waves a hand dismissively and sits

I made the mistake I got the driver to drop me at the front gate.
Nicely Oh, you have had a walk.
Horváth Yes.
Nicely Did you see the Renoirs on your way through the house?
Horváth No, I didn't, are they here?
Nicely No, no, paintings, the paintings.
Horváth Oh. No.
Nicely They're kind of fun. Look at them later.
Horváth Yes.

Silence. Nicely steals a look at his watch

Nicely Well. Did you have time to give our project a little thought?
Horváth Sure.
Nicely Any ideas? I know writing a sequel isn't as interesting as doing an
original, but there's a kind of discipline in it, you know?
Horváth Yes.
Nicely OK. Let's have it.
Horváth Well, I thought ... I mean, I was thinking about it quite a lot, to
find a different direction or so, and I think what we should do in this
one is we should see him ... he should fall in love with the chimpanzee.

Silence. Nicely looks at him, perplexed

Nicely Are you serious?
Horváth Sure.
Nicely Fall in love with the goddamn chimpanzee?
Horváth Yes. This is my most interesting idea.
Nicely Well, Ed, I don't deny it's interesting. A little too interesting I
would think for the Front Office.
Horváth Don't worry. I make everything all right in the end.
Nicely How?
Horváth Well: he marries the chimpanzee.

Nicely bursts out laughing. Horváth smiles

Nicely You don't really want to do this picture, do you?
Horváth No.
Nicely I don't blame you.
Horváth On the other hand, I need the money.

Silence. Nicely looks at his watch again, this time openly

Nicely Let me see what I can do. (*He gets up*) You want a swim?
Horváth What?

Nicely I'm afraid I have to go now. Would you like a swim?

Horváth (*getting up*) OK, sure, my pool's so small I only get to swim with one arm.

Nicely Everything's in the pool house. Oh. How long do you need?

Horváth Er, twenty minutes, half an hour.

Nicely OK, I'll send my chauffeur out for you in half an hour. He'll take you wherever you want to go.

Horváth Thank you.

Nicely Good to see you. I'll be in touch. (*He shakes hands with Horváth again and sets off across the lawn*)

Nicely exits

The Light begins to change to the underwater effect from the beginning of the play and to concentrate in a spot on Horváth

Horváth Well, I felt a bit of a fool, tell you the truth. But I was hot and it was a lovely pool, so I solemnly changed in the pool house and lowered myself gently in.

As he continues, the Young Man from the first scene of the play appears way downstage. He's wearing a black uniform and has a peaked cap under his arm. Moving with great deliberation, he puts the cap on, then brings out some dark glasses, which he settles on his nose and slowly buttons on a pair of black leather gloves. Eventually, he begins to move towards the centre of the stage

I splashed about a bit and then decided to do some serious swimming. But I hadn't done more than two or three lengths, when I ran head-first smack into a corner of the marble steps which led down into the centre of the pool. Everything went black. Later, there were violent struggles. I was aware of a great gash which had opened above one temple. Then, all of a sudden, through the blue-green rectangle above, I had a distorted glimpse of the rolling lawns, the obedient trees, the imposing ivy-covered walls, Eden paid for out of other men's dreams. A great peace stole over me. By the time the chauffeur arrived, looking as if he'd escaped from that new Cocteau picture, I was lying, comfortable as could be, on the bottom. The sun blazed down on us and on this Biblical city. As for me, dear friends, as for me, I was dead at last.

Horváth turns and looks at the Young Man for a moment, then turns and walks off

The spot snaps off and the Young Man stands looking down into the pool. His expression remains calm. Slow fade to Black-out

FURNITURE AND PROPERTY LIST

Only essential items are listed here but further dressing may be added at the director's discretion. Please read the Production Note on page v.

ACT I

SCENE 1

On stage: Nil

Off stage: Wicker chair, book for **Thomas (Stage Management)**

Personal: **Horváth:** wristwatch (worn throughout)
Young Man: glasses
Thomas Mann: round glasses (used throughout)
Harpo: tennis racquet with motor-horn on one end
Reporters: notebooks, pens
Photographers: cameras with flashguns and bulbs (practical)

SCENE 2

MONEY'S OFFICE
Strike: Wicker chair, book

Set: Desk. *On it:* telephones, slim folder
2 chairs

SCENE 3

THOMAS MANN'S BUNGALOW
Strike: Desk and contents
2 chairs

Set: 2 armchairs
Coffee-table. *On it:* thick manuscript, cigarettes, lighter, ashtray, glass of brandy, tray containing 2 cups, pot of coffee, sugar, milk etc.

SCENE 4

MONEY'S OFFICE
Strike: 2 armchairs
Coffee-table and contents

Set: Desk. *On it:* telephones, heavy black folder containing manuscript
2 chairs

SCENE 5

Strike: WARNER BROTHERS' COMMISSARY
Desk and contents
2 chairs

Set: Table. *On it:* cup of black coffee, book for **Helen**
Table. *On it:* cup of coffee for **Heinrich**
3 chairs

Off stage: Tray containing cup of coffee (**Horváth**)

Personal: **Heinrich:** round glasses (worn throughout)

SCENE 6

Strike: SALKA'S FRONT ROOM
2 tables and contents
3 chairs

Set: Long table. *On it:* candles, flower arrangements, dinner-place settings, glasses containing red wine, open bottles of red wine
Chairs

Off stage: Serving dish containing joint of roast beef (**Toni**)

Personal: **Thomas:** manuscript in pocket
Heinrich: speech in pocket

SCENE 7

Strike: HELEN'S APARTMENT
Long table and contents
Chairs

Set: Sofa
Table. *On it:* cigarettes, lighter, ashtray, fruit bowl containing apples

SCENE 8

On stage: As previous scene

Personal: **Brecht:** wristwatch and glasses (worn throughout), cigar

SCENE 9

Strike: HEINRICH MANN'S SITTING-ROOM
Sofa
Table and contents

Set: Armchair
Sofa
Coffee-table
Desk
Wastepaper basket

Off stage: Glass of red wine (**Nelly**)
Glass of red wine and open bottle (**Nelly**)

Scene 10

BRECHT'S GARDEN
Strike: Wine bottle and glasses
Off stage: Square of green linen (**Brecht**)
Personal: **Brecht:** small sign (brecht's garden) inside jacket, cigar

Scene 11

HEINRICH MANN'S SITTING-ROOM
On stage: As Scene 9
Off stage: Tray containing glasses and open bottle of wine (**Nelly**)
                 Birthday cake and lit candles (**Nelly**)

ACT II

Scene 1

"THE SLEEPING BEAUTY" BAR
On stage: Bar counter. *On it:* glasses, various bottles of wine, scotch etc., water,
                 ice
                 Table. *On it:* papers, glass of red wine for **Horváth**
                 Table. *On it:* glass of scotch on the rocks for **Angel**
                 3 chairs
Personal: **Hal:** cloth

Scene 2

"THE SLEEPING BEAUTY" BAR
On stage: As previous scene
Off stage: Open bottle of red wine, 2 glases (**Hal**)

Scene 3

THE BEACH
Strike: Bar counter and contents
                 2 tables and contents
                 3 chairs

Scene 4

HEINRICH MANN'S SITTING-ROOM
On stage: Sofa
                 Armchair
                 Coffee-table
                 Desk
                 Wastepaper basket
Off stage: Glass of red wine (**Nelly**)
Personal: **Lomakhin:** 2 large bundles of banknotes in pocket
                 Nelly: key

SCENE 5

SALKA'S FRONT ROOM

Strike: Sofa
Armchair
Coffee-table and contents

Set: Long table. *On it:* papers, pens etc.
Chairs

SCENE 6

HORVÁTH'S SITTING-ROOM

Strike: Long table and contents
Chairs

Set: Sofa
Table. *On it:* pot of coffee, sugar, milk, cups, saucers, spoons etc.

Off stage: Large banner: TWO FELLOW-DRAMATISTS REACH THE PART-
ING OF THE WAYS (**Brecht**)

Personal: **Brecht:** cigar, matches, piece of paper

SCENE 7

HEINRICH MANN'S SITTING-ROOM

Strike: Sofa
Table and contents

Set: Armchair
Sofa
Coffee-table
Desk. *On it:* carafe of water, glass. *In drawer:* bottle of pills
Wastepaper basket

SCENE 8

Strike: Armchair
Sofa
Coffee-table
Desk and contents
Wastepaper basket

Personal: **Brecht:** lighted cigar

SCENE 9

HEINRICH MANN'S BED-SITTING ROOM

On stage: Bed
Chair
Large wardrobe full of women's clothes including **Nelly's** red blouse

SCENE 10

	HELEN'S APARTMENT
Strike:	Bed
	Chair
	Large wardrobe
Set:	Sofa
	Table. *On it:* bottle of scotch, glasses, ice

SCENE 11

	A POOLSIDE
Strike:	Sofa
	Table and contents
Set:	2 canvas chairs
Personal:	**Nicely:** wristwatch
	Young Man: dark glasses

LIGHTING PLOT

Property fittings required: nil

Various interior and exterior settings

ACT I

To open:	Rippling submarine light	
Cue 1	Distant thunder *Change rippling light to street lamp effect*	(Page 1)
Cue 2	**Horváth:** "... with the hairdresser's." *Bring up lighting on crowd upstage*	(Page 2)
Cue 3	**Horváth:** "It was a pleasant evening." *Change to general evening light*	(Page 2)
Cue 4	As wind and rain effects start *Darken lighting downstage*	(Page 2)
Cue 5	**Young Man** moves C *Tree shadow effect* C	(Page 2)
Cue 6	**Horváth** moves downstage *Fade all except downstage lighting*	(Page 3)
Cue 7	**Horváth:** "Los Angeles!" *Circus lighting*	(Page 3)
Cue 8	**Horváth:** "... I dreamed of legendary encounters." *Bring up lighting on* **Thomas Mann**	(Page 4)
Cue 9	**Tarzan** and **Thomas Mann** exit *Cross fade to* **Chico** *and* **Harpo**	(Page 4)
Cue 10	**Chico:** "... he gotta very sneaky rhythm." *Bring up general lighting*	(Page 5)
Cue 11	Flashbulb pops *Camera flashes*	(Page 5)
Cue 12	**Garbo:** "Ve vant to be alone." *Camera flashes*	(Page 5)
Cue 13	**Garbo** and the media exit *Bring up normal California daytime lighting on* **Horváth** *downstage*	(Page 5)
Cue 14	**Horváth:** "... the reality was very different." *Change to interior effect on* **Money's** *office for* SCENE 2	(Page 6)
Cue 15	**Horváth** rises and moves downstage *Cross fade to follow spot on* **Horváth**	(Page 8)

Cue 16	**Horváth:** "... I ever spent with him alone." *Cross fade to interior lighting on Mann's bungalow for* SCENE 3	(Page 8)
Cue 17	**Horváth** gets up and moves downstage *Follow spot on* **Horváth**, *slow fade on bungalow area*	(Page 11)
Cue 18	**Horváth:** "I returned, quietly confident." *Cross fade to interior lighting on Money's office for* SCENE 4	(Page 11)
Cue 19	**Horváth** leaves the room *Cross fade to follow spot on* **Horváth**	(Page 13)
Cue 20	**Horváth:** "... treating their secretaries." *Cross fade to interior lighting on commissary area for* SCENE 5	(Page 14)
Cue 21	**Horváth** rises and moves downstage *Cross fade to follow spot on* **Horváth**	(Page 16)
Cue 22	**Horváth:** "... Garbo's writer, Salka Viertel." *Slow cross fade to Viertel's front room for* SCENE 6	(Page 17)
Cue 23	**Salka** rises to her feet *Black-out*	(Page 20)
Cue 24	To open Scene 7 *Follow spot on* **Horváth**	(Page 21)
Cue 25	**Horváth:** "... to improve my English." *Black-out. Pause, then bring up interior effect on apartment area*	(Page 21)
Cue 26	**Horváth** rises and is about to follow **Helen** *Snap on House Lights*	(Page 24)
Cue 27	**Horváth:** "... questions he didn't approve of." *Fade House Lights*	(Page 24)
Cue 28	**Brecht:** "I was afraid of that." *Cross fade to Mann's sitting-room for* SCENE 9	(Page 27)
Cue 29	**Heinrich, Nelly** and **Horváth** drink a toast *Cross fade to follow spot on* **Horváth**	(Page 30)
Cue 30	**Horváth:** "... an audience in Santa Monica." *Cross fade to lighting on* **Brecht**	(Page 30)
Cue 31	**Horváth:** "... able to work together." *Cross fade follow spot on* **Horváth**	(Page 32)
Cue 32	**Horváth:** "... better starts to the week." *Bring up interior lighting on Mann's sitting-room*	(Page 32)
Cue 33	**Horváth:** "... all those formidable Germans." *Fade follow spot*	(Page 33)
Cue 34	**Horváth:** "It's true to say ..." *Start slow fade*	(Page 35)
Cue 35	**Horváth** strolls off *Bring up House Lights*	(Page 35)

ACT II

To open:	Garish neon light show	
Cue 36	**Horváth:** "Donuts! Dentistry! Divorce!" *Black-out*	(Page 36)
Cue 37	**Horváth:** "Right, that's quite enough of that." *Bring up dim, interior lighting on bar area*	(Page 36)
Cue 38	**Brecht** gestures up to the lighting-box *Full white lighting*	(Page 37)
Cue 39	**Horváth** waves to the lighting-box *Return to dim interior lighting on bar area*	(Page 37)
Cue 40	**Hal** returns to the bar *Fade to Black-out, short pause, then bring up dim, interior lighting on bar area*	(Page 41)
Cue 41	**Horváth** exits *Fade to Black-out*	(Page 45)
Cue 42	To open SCENE 3 *Bring up exterior effect*	(Page 45)
Cue 43	**Helen** and **Horváth** stroll off *Cross fade to interior effect on sitting-room for SCENE 4*	(Page 47)
Cue 44	**Horváth** turns and moves abruptly downstage *Cross fade to follow spot on* **Horváth**	(Page 50)
Cue 45	**Horváth:** "... among the émigrés." *Cross fade to Salka's front room for SCENE 5*	(Page 51)
Cue 46	**Horváth** slips away downstage *Cross fade to follow spot on* **Horváth**	(Page 53)
Cue 47	Insistent pounding on front door *Cross fade to Horváth's sitting-room for SCENE 6*	(Page 53)
Cue 48	**Horváth** moves downstage *Cross fade to Mann's sitting-room for SCENE 7*	(Page 56)
Cue 49	**Horváth** takes **Nelly's** hand *Dim lighting*	(Page 58)
Cue 50	**Horváth** moves downstage *Follow spot on* **Horváth**	(Page 58)
Cue 51	**Horváth:** "... with a difference." *Strobe lighting on* **Heinrich** and **Nelly**	(Page 58)
Cue 52	**Horváth:** "... Nelly had just died." *Snap off strobe and all lighting except for spot on* **Horváth**	(Page 59)
Cue 53	**Horváth:** "... Activities Committee was ..." *Spot on* **Brecht**	(Page 60)
Cue 54	**Brecht:** "... never." *Snap off spot on* **Brecht**	(Page 60)

EFFECTS PLOT

ACT I

Cue 1	**Horváth:** "... the water-polo team." *Distant thunder*	(Page 1)
Cue 2	**Horváth:** "So." (*He pauses*) *Very distant thunder, light wind rising*	(Page 1)
Cue 3	**Horváth** strolls across the stage humming *Wind rising, followed by rain effect*	(Page 2)
Cue 4	**Horváth:** "... this storm." *Thunderclap, wind increasing in intensity*	(Page 2)
Cue 5	As **Horváth** describes sounds *Tree branch snapping off in wind followed by second branch falling*	(Page 2)
Cue 6	**Young Man** topples forward *Snap off all effects*	(Page 2)
Cue 7	**Horváth:** "... into an elevator." *Birdsong*	(Page 3)
Cue 8	**Horváth:** "... Führer's latest thinking." *Hitler speech as in text*	(Page 3)
Cue 9	**Horváth** exits *Wagner's Prelude to* Lohengrin *plays quietly*	(Page 4)
Cue 10	**Tarzan:** "... you Thomas Mann." *Snap off Wagner*	(Page 4)

Cue 11	**Harpo** strums on his tennis racquet *Four opening notes of "Verklärte Nacht"*	(Page 5)
Cue 12	**Money:** "Oh, yeah, good." *Telephone*	(Page 6)
Cue 13	**Money:** "Oh." *2nd telephone*	(Page 7)
Cue 14	**Horváth:** "Excuse me?" *3rd telephone*	(Page 8)
Cue 15	**Horváth:** "Am I bent?" *Telephone*	(Page 12)
Cue 16	**Money:** "We're not ready for it." *Telephone*	(Page 13)
Cue 17	**Horváth:** "... I found myself an employee of:" *Signature tune from* Looney Tunes	(Page 14)
Cue 18	**Horváth:** "... treating their secretaries." *Fade* Looney Tunes *music*	(Page 14)
Cue 19	**Horváth:** "... born to be a writer." *Screech of brakes and muffled thud*	(Page 27)

ACT II

Cue 20	To open SCENE 1 Sunset Boulevard *music*	(Page 36)
Cue 21	**Horváth:** "Donuts! Dentistry! Divorce!" *Snap off music*	(Page 36)
Cue 22	**Horváth** concentrates on his papers for a moment *Screech of brakes*	(Page 41)
Cue 23	To open SCENE 3 *Roar of the surf. Continue throughout scene*	(Page 45)
Cue 24	**Horváth:** "... you know, meetings." *Orchestral version of "Und Sonst Gar Nichts" and doorbell as* *in text for* SCENE 4 *opening*	(Page 47)
Cue 25	As **Heinrich** crosses to the door *Fade music and punctuate scene with sound of passing traffic*	(Page 47)
Cue 26	**Horváth:** "Well, I, well, no." *Doorbell*	(Page 48)
Cue 27	**Lomakhin:** "Yes." *Sound of key in front door*	(Page 49)
Cue 28	To open SCENE 6 *Insistent pounding*	(Page 53)
Cue 29	**Horváth:** "All over Hollywood ..." *"America the Beautiful" and "Internationale" as described in* text	(Page 59)

Cue 30   **Horváth:** "... gratified to the full."   (Page 59)
            Cut music

Cue 31   **Horváth:** "Bertolt Brecht."   (Page 60)
            Robert E. Stripling sequence as in text

Cue 32   **Horváth** shakes his head, amazed   (Page 62)
            "Und Sonst Gar Nichts" plays very quietly

Cue 33   **Horváth:** "... I'd never owned."   (Page 62)
            Fade music

PROJECTION PLOT

Please note that a licence issued by Samuel French Ltd to perform this play DOES NOT include permission to use any copyright material which the projection sequences may involve. Should such material be used application must be made to the copyright holders concerned.

ACT I

ACT II